SOME SLAVES

OF

FAUQUIER COUNTY, VIRGINIA

VOLUME IV: MASTER INDEX

WILL BOOKS 1–31

1759–1869

COMPILED BY

Sandra Barlau

HERITAGE BOOKS
2014

HERITAGE BOOKS

AN IMPRINT OF HERITAGE BOOKS, INC.

Books, CDs, and more—Worldwide

For our listing of thousands of titles see our website
at
www.HeritageBooks.com

Published 2014 by
HERITAGE BOOKS, INC.
Publishing Division
5810 Ruatan Street
Berwyn Heights, Md. 20740

Copyright © 2014 Sandra Barlau

Heritage Books by the author:

Some Slaves of Fauquier County, Virginia, Volume I: Will Books 1–10, 1759–1829
Some Slaves of Fauquier County, Virginia; Volume II: Will Books 11–20, 1829–1847
Some Slaves of Fauquier County, Virginia, Volume III: Will Books 21–31, 1847–1869
Some Slaves of Fauquier County, Virginia;
Volume IV: Master Index, Will Books 1–31, 1759–1869

Cover portrait: Mary Timbers Harrison

International Standard Book Numbers
Paperbound: 978-0-7884-5584-1
Clothbound: 978-0-7884-6018-0

To those who are searching for their own "Mildred Timbers"

TABLE OF CONTENTS

PREFACE

The idea for these books originated when I decided it was necessary to read the Fauquier County, Virginia Will Books 11-20 from 1827 to 1843. Alexander Jeffries' estate sold a girl, Mildred, to his son Eli Jeffries in 1844. (Will Book 19, pg 99). The question was how did he acquire her? It is not known how Mildred Timbers, my second great–grandmother, became a slave of Alexander Jeffries. Was she willed to him or to his wife? Did he purchase her at a sale? Was her mother already his property when she was born?

Mildred would have been approximately two years old in 1829, the start of Will Book 11. I would have to read every page of every Will Book to find whether she was willed or sold to Alexander Jeffries in an estate sale. Since reading the Will Books entailed a great deal of work I decided to cull the owners and their slaves and present it in book form. How I wished I had these books in hand during my own research! It would have taken only a few minutes to read through them instead of several months reading the microfilm rolls.

What began as curiosity quickly turned into a passion as I learned more and more about my family. I even met cousins that I did not know about previously.

INTRODUCTION

This Master Index allows you to compare, and follow through the years, the changes in surnames and family descendents from each Will Book. It is easier to research the slave owners but it is possible to follow some slaves from one owner to another.

Having all the indexes in this one volume simplifies and defines which Will Books you need to explore. Many times an Account or Will was recorded by the court years after it had been prepared. Here are two examples: Charles Martin's committee account was dated from 27 Dec 1853 to 12 Aug 1854 but recorded in Will Book 27 on 18 Feb 1857, not Will Book 25. The guardian account of D.H.C. Beale has dates ranging from 1 July 1851 – 1 Jan 1855 but was recorded in Will Book 31 on 23 Sept 1867 rather than Will Book 25 or 26.

First names were standardized in order to make your index search easier. When you go to the original Will Books be aware that different spellings were used. Be creative in looking for first names: Rowzee (Rosy), Ausker (Oscar), Fillis (Phillis), Veanus (Venus) etc. Sometimes the written nn could be rr and many times S resembles L. The use of the term (sic) is not used for these reasons. The same name can also appear more than once on a page under different owners.

The quality of the films varies and some microfilm copies were difficult to read. Because of this some of the entries have only a few letters separated with a blank space such as Marj__i_. It would be a good idea to peruse the entire index. You may recognize a name with another spelling. I apologize for any inaccurate transcriptions.

I would like to thank the Family History Library at Salt Lake City for providing the microfilms and the San Diego Family History Center for the use of their microfilm readers and for their gracious volunteers.

VOLUME I

WILL BOOKS 1 – 10

1759 – 1829

_asco, 92
_hirza, 124
A. Sally, 92
A_ile, 100
A_ow, 92
Aan__, 133
Aaron, 7, 15, 16, 34, 42, 45, 52,
  53, 54, 66, 73, 77, 80, 81, 82,
  84, 86, 88, 103, 108, 109,
  113, 114, 133, 139, 143, 154,
  160, 167, 174, 177, 179, 186,
  188, 193, 195, 196, 197, 201,
  207, 208
Abby, 103, 137, 146, 151
Abel, 3, 17, 42, 56, 86, 87, 112,
  143, 145, 147, 170, 171, 179
ABELL: Alexander, 105;
  Ephraim, 66, 103, 105, 115;
  James H., 105; John, 105;
  Nancy, 105; Polly, 105;
  Robert, 105; Susanna, 105;
  Thornton, 105
Abey, 81
Abigail, 99, 160
Abigille, 98
Abner, 64, 93, 103, 204
Abraham, 9, 17, 35, 64, 67, 73,
  79, 81, 86, 88, 98, 99, 118,
  123, 124, 128, 130, 133, 147,
  151, 152, 155, 158, 161, 163,
  172, 173, 174, 177, 178, 184,
  190, 191, 195, 198, 200, 202,
  208
Abralom, 133
Abram, 1, 2, 5, 68, 74, 90, 113,
  116, 117, 138, 143, 154, 156,
  157, 188, 197
Adaline, 132, 170

Adam, 1, 2, 3, 4, 5, 9, 10, 11,
  16, 17, 29, 32, 33, 35, 41, 43,
  63, 66, 75, 77, 79, 86, 87, 90,
  91, 93, 102, 104, 105, 115,
  118, 119, 123, 124, 126, 128,
  129, 134, 143, 151, 154, 163,
  165, 170, 196, 200, 206
ADAM: Sarah, 93
ADAMS: Charles, 206; George,
  86; James, 85, 86; John, 23;
  Josiah, 86; Littleton, 86;
  Samuel, 165; Sarah, 86, 87,
  93, 139; Thomas, 86, 139;
  Turner, 140; Willis, 118
ADAMS Jr.: Thomas, 172
Adda, 123, 195
Addison, 157
Adelaide, 160
Adeline, 190
Adeliza, 117
Adesson, 142
ADIE: Margaret, 38
Admiral, 127
Ady, 20
Aga, 107
Agar, 9
Agatha, 24, 65, 74, 80, 91, 102,
  173, 174
Agatha Nelly, 4
Agg, 79, 94, 149
Agga, 16, 18, 35, 66, 75, 77, 85,
  103, 107, 109, 112, 124, 129,
  131
Aggais, 71
Aggy, 19, 45, 51, 52, 53, 58,
  66, 67, 72, 77, 79, 80, 85, 87,
  89, 93, 100, 104, 105, 107,

1

Ampa, 76
Ampy, 100
Amy, 10, 15, 20, 22, 35, 36, 37,
   39, 40, 42, 44, 51, 53, 57, 64,
   73, 75, 77, 81, 82, 91, 107,
   111, 112, 120, 122, 125, 141,
   153, 155, 156, 157, 159, 162,
   163, 168, 170, 173, 174, 175,
   180, 188
Anarchy, 166
Anderson, 137, 140, 194
ANDERSON: Ezekiel, 139;
   Presley, 76
Andrew, 74, 79, 99, 110, 113,
   153, 162, 188, 189, 195
Angeline, 201
Angelo, 13
Angelos, 37
Angilla, 10, 11
Anistaid, 54
Ann, 20, 22, 24, 28, 47, 49, 63,
   65, 74, 80, 81, 97, 110, 111,
   112, 114, 120, 127, 131, 141,
   145, 158, 159, 165, 167, 174,
   184, 189, 192, 194, 196, 198,
   203
Ann Mariah, 159, 162
Ann Smith, 10
Anna, 39, 51, 57, 69, 73, 81, 83,
   93, 94, 101, 104, 112, 123, 132,
   150, 160, 177, 188, 192, 194,
   206
Anna Maria, 173, 183
Annaka, 128
Anncey, 57
Anne, 68, 83, 88, 124, 131, 147,
   155, 179
Annie, 77, 134
Anny, 83, 88, 89, 142, 171,
   173, 177
Ano_, 137
Anos, 117
Anthony, 1, 2, 9, 12, 13, 16, 17,
   22, 27, 28, 31, 35, 39, 40, 49,
   50, 55, 56, 58, 59, 64, 72, 75,

79, 81, 86, 87, 90, 91, 92, 99,
   101, 102, 103, 109, 110, 111,
   117, 119, 122, 123, 127, 128,
   129, 131, 133, 155, 160, 172,
   173, 178, 188, 194, 202, 206
Ara, 153
Arabella, 194
Arch, 18, 19, 41, 66, 120, 132,
   155, 156, 162, 173, 199
Archibald, 124, 129, 146, 149,
   162
Archus, 71
Archy, 188
Arene, 179
Argile, 85
Argyle, 85
Ariel, 63
Armistead, 29, 30, 31, 42, 43,
   45, 69, 77, 80, 84, 93, 102,
   103, 106, 109, 111, 112, 117,
   118, 119, 121, 124, 128, 129,
   130, 131, 137, 138, 139, 147,
   151, 153, 159, 160, 166, 169,
   170, 172, 178, 180, 186, 188,
   205
Armlir, 66
Armstrong, 10, 12
ARNOLD: Elijah, 100;
   Humphrey, 36, 38; John,
   103; Mary, 149; Mrs., 38
Arrick, 162
Art, 74
Arthur, 66, 158, 183, 194, 203
Artry, 38
ASBERRY: William, 44
ASH: Elizabeth, 11; Frances,
   180; Francis, 11, 12, 76;
   George, 180; Mary, 118;
   Nancy, 86; William, 118,
   151
ASH Sr.: George, 91, 92
ASHBERRY: Jane, 44
Ashby, 49, 72, 97
ASHBY: Alexander, 39;
   Benjamin, 39; Capt. John,

3

4

100, 101, 117, 131, 134, 137, 182

Betta, 116

Betty, 4, 6, 8, 17, 20, 21, 22, 29, 31, 35, 36, 38, 39, 51, 52, 53, 54, 55, 56, 57, 58, 59, 60, 61, 62, 63, 65, 66, 67, 71, 73, 74, 76, 80, 81, 82, 83, 85, 86, 87, 90, 91, 93, 94, 95, 98, 99, 105, 111, 113, 114, 115, 116, 117, 118, 119, 120, 122, 123, 124, 126, 127, 128, 129, 132, 133, 134, 137, 139, 140, 142, 143, 144, 148, 149, 153, 154, 157, 158, 160, 164, 166, 169, 172, 174, 175, 178, 181, 183, 186, 188, 189, 192, 193, 195, 196, 197, 199

Betty Brink, 11

Betty Burk, 12

Betty Cook, 127

Betty Jackson, 127

Betty Jr., 111

Betty Sr., 111

Beverly, 62, 117, 123, 156, 160, 163, 166, 174, 192, 193, 200, 205

Bezzel, 118

Bibb, 111, 112

Bibby, 50

BICE: Ann Elizabeth, 169

Bick, 46

Bigg, 61

Bill, 21, 34, 57, 70, 73, 74, 77, 83, 89, 98, 99, 101, 102, 103, 104, 107, 111, 113, 120, 121, 124, 132, 133, 134, 141, 149, 156, 160, 162, 163, 167, 172, 173, 174, 178, 179, 182, 185, 186, 194, 203, 206, 207, 208

BILLINGS: James, 100

BILLINGSBY: Clement, 50, 59, 83; Elizabeth, 83; James, 63, 83, 95

BILLINGSLEY: Betsey, 76; Clement, 76; James, 76; John, 76

Billy, 5, 31, 41, 42, 45, 49, 53, 58, 60, 61, 64, 66, 67, 68, 69, 78, 80, 86, 90, 98, 100, 107, 109, 110, 111, 122, 126, 127, 130, 132, 134, 137, 141, 143, 148, 153, 158, 166, 178, 181, 184, 188, 194, 201, 203

Billy Robinson, 158

Billy Sr, 201

Billy W, 188

Bird, 64, 160

BISHOP: Josiah, 157

Bitsey, 35

Bitt, 31

Black, 149

Black James, 81, 82

Black Joe, 82

Black Smith, 148

BLACKBURN: Judith, 35

BLACKMORE: James, 180

Blackwell, 133

BLACKWELL: Ann, 72, 192; Ann Grayson, 38, 39; Capt. William, 33; Elizabeth, 12, 80, 97; Franca, 193; John, 168, 174, 193; John E, 193; John E., 175; Joseph, 192; Samuel, 39, 121, 182, 186; William, 12, 43, 72, 174, 193

BLACKWELL Sr.: Joseph, 33

Blake, 151

BLAKE: Elizabeth, 146; William, 146

BLAND: Benjamin, 7; Catherine, 35; Jackey, 23; James, 85; Jane, 73, 86; Mary, 23, 35; Thomas, 35, 36

Boatswain, 37

Bob, 1, 2, 6, 7, 11, 12, 13, 15, 16, 18, 24, 31, 32, 33, 34, 36,

43, 45, 50, 51, 52, 54, 62, 64, 66, 68, 70, 71, 73, 75, 82, 87, 98, 99, 102, 103, 105, 106, 110, 111, 117, 119, 120, 122, 123, 127, 129, 132, 138, 140, 144, 148, 150, 152, 158, 160, 169, 170, 172, 180, 189, 190, 192, 194, 200

Bob Cook, 181

Bob Jr., 133

BOGGESS: Jeremiah, 8; Richard, 8; Thomas, 8

BOGGS: Thomas, 8

Bookrey, 17

Boran, 47

BOSEWELL: William, 9

Bossin, 44

BOTELER: Joseph, 190

Boutwell, 110

BOWEN: Alexander, 89; Elizabeth, 98, 165, 166; Frances, 89; James, 121, 125; John, 89; Mary, 121; Peter, 121; Sarah, 88; Stephen, 88, 89, 98, 166

BOWENER: George, 94

BOWER: Betsy, 124; Francis, 186; Peter, 62, 64, 123; Susannah, 62; William, 61, 124

BOWMAN: George, 113; Peter, 113

BOWMER: Burkett, 120; Charles, 120; Eliza, 120; George, 83; Peter, 114, 120; Polly, 120; Susannah, 120

BOYD: James, 82

BRADFORD: Alice, 102; Ann, 43; Anne, 1; Benjamin, 45; Charles, 102, 196; Daniel, 60, 63, 196; Elizabeth William, 2; Enoch, 102, 115, 196; Fielding, 102, 115, 196; Frances, 185; Frederick AC, 185; Harvey Herms, 185;

Issachar Harrison, 185; John, 60, 102, 196; Joseph, 105; Louisa Rowena, 185; Mary, 27; Sally, 116; Sarah, 47, 60, 102, 196; Simon, 60, 102, 115, 116, 196; Theodrick, 184; Thomas Grayson, 184; William, 1, 32, 60, 102, 184, 201

BRADLEY: David, 202

BRADY: Betsey, 99; Elizabeth, 99, 161, 166; Helen, 99; Jenney, 99; Joseph, 99, 101; Mahala, 99; Thornton, 99

BRAGG: William, 208

BRAHAN: John, 13, 14; Lettice, 13

BRAND: William, 168

BRAWN: Thomas, 91

Braxton, 156

Bray, 17, 103

BRENT: Alexander, 88; Ann, 61; Christopher Neale, 61; Elizabeth, 139; Elizabeth Mary, 61; Hannah, 61; Hugh, 142; Mary Waddy, 61; William, 61, 62

Briant, 23

Bridget, 50, 129

BRIDGEWATERS: Abraham, 141

BRIGGS: Robert, 113

Brister, 79, 98, 101, 104, 145, 153, 193

Bristoe, 9, 10, 11, 74, 133, 147

Bristol, 43, 99, 122

Bristow, 184

Britain, 75

Britton, 77

BRONAUGH: John, 15, 18; Margret, 15; Mary Ann, 15; Mary Mason, 15; William, 15

BRONAUNT: Sarah, 15

Brooke, 108, 205

BROOKE: Anne, 49; Col. H., 78; Col. Humphrey, 68; Francis, 49, 67, 86, 106, 115; George, 49; Humphrey, 67; Humphry, 78; Lucy, 49; Martin, 106, 114, 115; Matthew, 49, 78; Matthew W., 106, 114, 115; Milly, 67; Nancy, 78; Thomas, 114
Brooked, 103
Brookery, 39
Brookes, 66
BROOKS: Nancy, 77
BROWN: Dixon, 21; Elizabeth, 98; Enoch, 93; Mary, 29, 33; Molly, 49; Sally, 123; Thomas, 177; Winifred, 189
BROWN, Jr: Daniel, 184, 198
BROWNE: Enoch J., 104
Brownell, 162
BROWNING: Caleb, 38
BRUCE: Alexander, 143, 190; Baley, 197
Bryan, 2
Bryant, 102, 107, 137, 140, 168, 174, 175, 193, 200
Buck, 45, 118
Buckner, 68, 160
BUCKNER: Thornton, 45
Bucye, 73
BULL: Margaret, 121
BULLETT: Joseph, 41; Thomas, 15
BULLITT: Barshiba Norman, 41; Benjamin, 1, 4; Elizabeth, 4; Sarah, 4
Burchell, 116
BURDETT: Mary, 41
Burgess, 76
BURGESS: Dawson, 6; Edward, 74, 146, 148; Fanny, 146; Frances, 149; Francis, 6; Garner, 38, 82; James, 57, 65, 74; John, 74, 146; Peggy, 74; Sara, 146;

Sarah, 182, 189; Susannah, 74; William, 149
Burgun, 22
BURNLEY: John, 103
Burr, 167, 184
Burrell, 92
Bursheba, 9, 18
Burton, 145, 147, 153, 179
Burwell, 124, 153, 163, 165, 203, 207
BURWELL: Jephtha, 207
Bush, 39
Bushrod, 192
BUTLER: Alice, 149; Joseph, 142; Laurence, 149, 180
BYRNE: Ann, 130; Darby B, 181; Darby B., 137

C__ina, 10
Cabb, 67
Caesar, 4, 11, 13, 18, 23, 45, 54, 68, 75, 77, 87, 89, 108, 114, 118, 141, 153, 154, 160, 161, 170, 185, 192
CAFFREY: Baley M., 120; John M., 120
Cage, 81, 106, 130, 173, 206
Cailey, 153
Cain, 53, 117
Cainer, 54
CAITLICH: Charles, 100
Caleb, 6, 8, 91, 92, 189
CALMES: Lucy, 11
CALVERT: George, 208
Caly, 65, 69, 144
Cambrick, 90
Camilla, 109
Campbell, 195
CAMPBELL: Catherine, 29; Hugh R., 125, 156
Can__, 104
Cane, 128
Canor, 21
Cany, 49
Captain, 166

8

Carberry, 93
CARDLITCH: Lucy, 179
Carey, 181
Cariar, 120
Carline, 162
Carlos, 194
Carly, 167
Carner, 138, 139
Carol, 105
Carol (Carl?), 93
Caroline, 42, 73, 102, 103, 105, 107, 108, 110, 114, 121, 122, 130, 132, 137, 139, 141, 155, 158, 164, 167, 170, 172, 174, 178, 181, 182, 183, 187, 188, 192, 194, 200, 202, 203, 206
Carr: James, 12
CARR: Caldwell, 208; Joseph, 206; Peter, 208
Carrell, 105
CARRELL: Sanford, 15
CARROL: Sandford, 46
CARROLL: Anna, 37
Carter, 88, 123, 133, 152, 185, 197, 200, 201
CARTER: Edward E., 155; George, 132, 134, 191; James P, 181; John F., 151; Judith, 131; Moore F, 180, 201, 206; Moore F., 158; Patsy, 132; Peter, 36; Polly, 132; Westward, 132; William F., 155; Winefred, 132
CARTLITCH: Charles, 106
Carty, 167
Cary, 27
Cass, 89
Cassa, 39
Cassandria, 56
Cassius, 89, 109
Caster, 46
Castle, 9, 17
Cate, 2, 6, 7, 9, 10, 11, 12, 13, 17, 20, 21, 22, 24, 29, 35, 37,

38, 39, 41, 42, 45, 46, 50, 52, 53, 54, 57, 60, 61, 62, 64, 66, 68, 69, 71, 76, 77, 85, 88, 89, 90, 93, 98, 104, 105, 109, 116, 118, 128, 133, 160
Catena, 21
Catherine, 28, 53, 65, 84, 91, 100, 118, 119, 133, 160, 207
CATLETT: Betty, 16; Dolly Massie, 143; John, 15, 16; Thomas, 140
Cato, 45, 70, 195
Catt, 72
CATTLET: Elizabeth, 101; Robert, 101; Sarah, 101
CATTLETT: Elizabeth, 15
Caty, 109, 126, 142, 144, 150, 156, 157, 171, 173, 194, 195, 199, 200, 206
CAVE: John, 53, 90; Rhody, 53, 90; Sally, 90; Samuel, 53, 90; Sarah, 53; Thomas, 53, 84, 90
CAVIELL: Elizabeth, 14; Sanford, 14
Cealey, 208
Ceasor, 82
Cecelia, 73, 123, 193, 195
Cecilia, 160
Cedar Run Jack, 130
Ceily, 174
Celah, 69, 101, 110
Cele, 146
Celia, 20, 21, 33, 38, 53, 57, 58, 66, 71, 73, 80, 93, 97, 99, 102, 116, 121, 122, 128, 142, 143, 145, 154, 156, 157, 158, 165, 166, 183, 188, 190, 192, 193, 195
Celia Martin, 68
Celie, 162
Celler, 66
Cely, 148, 195
Centiffy, 124
Ceny, 194

9

Cereny, 55
Ceslia, 70
Cetle, 115
CHAMBERLAYN: James, 13, 22
CHANCELLOR: Samuel, 201
Chandler, 36, 37, 123, 141, 194
Chandler Fowke, 45
CHANNELES: James, 57
Chapman, 64
CHAPMAN: George, 119, 196; John, 119; Nathaniel, 119; Pearson, 119; Susanna, 119; Thomas, 19
Chardle, 101
Charity, 7, 10, 27, 47, 50, 51, 58, 59, 60, 62, 69, 76, 81, 82, 93, 103, 108, 113, 115, 121, 126, 129, 133, 138, 144, 145, 147, 153, 156, 162, 167, 178, 179, 180, 188, 192, 196, 200, 201, 204, 207
Charles, 1, 8, 10, 11, 12, 13, 14, 15, 16, 17, 18, 20, 22, 23, 29, 31, 32, 33, 35, 36, 37, 38, 39, 40, 41, 42, 44, 50, 53, 57, 58, 59, 61, 62, 64, 65, 66, 68, 69, 70, 71, 72, 73, 74, 76, 79, 80, 82, 84, 88, 89, 90, 92, 93, 94, 97, 98, 99, 100, 101, 102, 109, 110, 111, 113, 115, 116, 119, 121, 122, 123, 124, 125, 126, 127, 128, 129, 130, 133, 134, 137, 139, 140, 141, 143, 146, 148, 150, 154, 156, 157, 159, 160, 163, 164, 165, 166, 168, 169, 170, 173, 178, 179, 181, 183, 184, 185, 188, 189, 190, 192, 194, 195, 198, 202, 203, 204, 205, 206, 207
Charles Dolan, 10
Charles Henry, 149, 185, 190
Charley, 98
Charlotta, 67

Charlotte, 10, 20, 22, 27, 28, 31, 34, 35, 42, 43, 50, 51, 52, 53, 57, 59, 60, 61, 62, 65, 66, 67, 68, 69, 70, 72, 75, 80, 81, 86, 87, 94, 102, 103, 104, 105, 106, 107, 109, 110, 111, 112, 113, 114, 117, 118, 119, 120, 122, 123, 124, 125, 129, 134, 137, 139, 142, 143, 144, 145, 146, 148, 149, 151, 152, 153, 154, 156, 159, 160, 164, 166, 169, 170, 171, 173, 174, 178, 179, 184, 186, 188, 190, 193, 195, 201, 203, 204, 205, 207
Charlotte Grace, 97
Charlotte Jr., 112
Chasity, 28, 186
Chassley, 111
Chatsworth, 188
Chelsey, 88
Chester, 81, 83
CHEW: Richard, 189
CHILD: Alexander, 183, 193; Ann, 107
Chilten, 201
CHILTEN: William, 53
Chilton, 155, 173, 174, 192
CHILTON: Charles, 42, 59, 73; Doc Samuel, 186; Elizabeth, 190; George, 42, 88; George MA, 193; John, 17, 42; Joseph, 42, 140; Lucy, 42; Mark A., 174; Mary Ellin, 88; Nancy, 43; Orrick, 42; Samuel, 186; Stephen, 183; Susanna, 42; Thomas, 42; William, 13, 42
China, 49, 50, 137, 140
CHINN: Ann, 159; Ann R., 139; Ann Richards, 152; Charles, 34; Christopher, 34; Hugh, 139, 142, 158; John, 8; Leth, 34; Margaret, 118; Mary, 159; Mary Ingles,

116; Patty, 152; Polly I., 139; Richard, 159; Sidney, 139, 159; Susan, 139, 152, 159; Susanna, 45; Sydney, 152; Thomas, 142
CHINN Jr.: Thomas, 142
CHINN Sr.: Thomas, 142
Chloe, 13, 37, 42, 50, 51, 53, 85, 100, 110, 111, 120, 123, 125, 128, 132, 144, 159, 166, 169, 172, 175, 179, 187, 194, 196
Chris, 34
Christina, 207
Christopher, 124, 155
CHUNN: John Thomas, 78; Martha, 78; Peregrigine, 116; Perigine, 62
CHURCHILL: John, 49
Cib, 145
Cidd, 72
Cilla, 44
Cillah, 101
Ciller, 58, 85
Cimor, 203
Cinah, 160
Cindar, 185
Cintha, 133
Cipio, 3
CLAGGETT: Samuel, 157
Clamina, 62, 116, 123
Clancy, 51
Clara, 45, 102, 107, 124, 125, 141, 159, 167, 174, 207
Clare, 71
Clarinda, 83, 90
Clarissa, 74, 138, 146
Clarisy, 84
Clark, 161, 174, 184, 201
CLARK: Benjamin, 52; Chloe, 120; Mary, 171; Thomas, 52
Clarke, 168
CLARKE: Benjamin, 120, 122; Thornton, 202

CLARKSON: Henry, 88; Marian M.M., 159; Milly, 77; William, 141
Clary, 22, 28, 51, 53, 60, 62, 64, 65, 66, 67, 69, 74, 75, 79, 81, 95, 98, 104, 106, 114, 116, 123, 125, 143, 146, 162, 165, 169
CLAXON: Thomas, 92
CLAXTON: Dully, 180; James, 95; Jeremiah, 95, 99; Jesse, 177; Jessee, 177; John P., 171; John Peyton, 95; Pope, 95, 99, 182, 190; Richard, 95; William, 95
Clay, 153
Clayton, 194
Clele, 92
Clem, 105, 109, 118, 195
Clemeany, 64
Clement, 128
CLERK: John Scott, 33
CLEVELAND: Levy, 169; Lucy, 54
Clinton, 62, 67, 81
Cloe, 4, 5, 50, 52, 76, 84, 85, 88, 93, 117, 127, 143, 145, 147, 153, 154, 157, 168, 172, 174, 175, 179, 181, 193
COCKERILLE: Sally, 207
COCKRELL: Hezekiah, 129
Coder, 188
Codger, 30
COLBERT: Lanta, 165
Cole, 166
Colman, 148
COLOIN: Richard, 192
COMBS: Benjamin, 159; Ennis, 55, 203; John, 24; Margret, 55; Sarah, 21; Seth, 159, 187, 203; William R, 203
COMBS Jr: John, 21
Condelia, 133
Congga, 74

Conrad, 192
CONWAY: Charlotte, 199; James, 29; Peter, 199; Thomas, 29; William, 29
Cook, 13, 22, 90, 111
COOK: Charles, 99; John, 152; Mrs., 152
Cooke, 88
COOKE: John, 144; Littleton, 23; Nancy, 203
COOKSEY: Mary, 118
Cooper, 22, 133, 142
COPPAGE: Elizabeth, 3; Hannah, 117; John, 3; Sally, 3; William, 3, 89
COPPEDGE: Mary, 87; William, 87
Corace, 195
CORBIN: Elisha Hall, 12; Hannah, 12; Martha, 12; Mrs., 165
CORDER: John, 112
Coreas, 30
Corin, 73
CORLEY: Frances, 167; James, 167; Minoah, 170
CORMETT: Richard R., 120
Cornelia Ann, 151
Cornelian, 151
Cornelius, 160, 165
CORNWELL: Ann, 146, 149, 151, 207; Jacob, 207; Lucy, 207; Mary, 207; Peter, 14, 16; Peyton, 146; Ruth, 146; Sarah Ann, 14
CORNWELL Jr: Mary, 207
CORNWELL Sr: Mary, 207
COSBY: Lewis, 127
COULSTON: Edward, 150
COURTNEY: Elizabeth, 110; Sarah, 123
COWERT: Lantee, 165; Sally, 165
COWLES: William T, 180

COX: Abraham, 72; Ann, 72; Elenor, 60, 61; Elizabeth, 72; William, 72; Zachariah, 72
CRAIG: James, 64; Rev. James, 73
Craven, 161, 168, 174, 184, 190, 198, 201
Crawford, 4, 153, 170, 205
CRAWLEY: W, 201
CRENSHAW: Caty, 121; Dulley, 103
CRESSWELL: Elizabeth, 207
Crib, 45
Cril, 162
CRIMM: Caty, 71
Cris, 50
Crispen, 178, 179
Criss, 19, 70, 160
CRISTA: Charles, 140
CROCKETT: James, 73
CROSBY: George, 29, 59, 95, 97; Jno., 95
CRUMP: Benjamin, 130, 139; George, 35, 40, 130; John, 130; Lucy, 46; Nancy, 130; Patsy, 130; Reuben, 130; Travis, 130; William, 130
Cudjir Hannah, 20
Cue, 49
Cuff, 24, 31, 84
Cuffy, 162
Culray, 151
Cumber, 30
Cumbo, 79, 97
Cumloo, 74
CUMMINS: Daniel, 163; John, 207; Williams, 207
CUNDIFF: Isaac, 63
Cupid, 23, 28, 32
CURTICE: Charlotte, 52
CURTIS: George, 158; John, 75
Cyne, 12
Cyntha, 139
Cynthia, 59, 65, 66, 80, 104, 141

Cyprus, 17
Cyrus, 58, 64, 72, 73, 117, 118, 120, 122, 128, 129, 131, 132, 156, 160, 174, 175, 179, 206
Cyrus Jr., 133
Cytha, 65

DADE: Mrs., 21
Daisy, 204
Dangerfield, 159, 163, 174, 197, 201
Daniel, 1, 2, 3, 5, 7, 9, 10, 11, 14, 15, 17, 18, 19, 20, 22, 27, 28, 30, 31, 32, 35, 37, 38, 40, 41, 45, 46, 47, 48, 52, 54, 56, 57, 58, 59, 61, 62, 64, 65, 66, 67, 68, 69, 70, 72, 73, 74, 75, 76, 79, 80, 84, 87, 88, 89, 90, 91, 92, 93, 94, 95, 97, 98, 99, 101, 103, 105, 106, 108, 110, 111, 112, 114, 115, 116, 117, 118, 119, 122, 124, 129, 130, 131, 133, 137, 138, 139, 140, 144, 147, 149, 150, 152, 153, 159, 161, 163, 164, 170, 171, 173, 174, 178, 182, 188, 189, 190, 194, 195, 196, 199, 200, 204, 206, 208
Daphne, 10, 11, 29, 30, 41, 61, 62, 70, 112, 131, 137, 140, 144, 145, 147, 179, 184, 192, 204
Darby, 53
Darcus, 119
Dario, 182
Dark, 9, 180
Darkey, 32, 41, 61, 76, 89, 107, 110, 133, 161, 168, 173, 174, 179, 184, 198
DARNAL: Katharine, 1
DARNALL: Caty, 47, 112; Jeremiah, 46, 47, 53, 112; Rosamond, 47
Darwin, 121

David, 10, 18, 19, 24, 30, 31, 35, 41, 45, 47, 50, 53, 55, 57, 61, 62, 63, 64, 65, 66, 67, 74, 75, 79, 81, 87, 88, 91, 99, 105, 106, 113, 117, 118, 122, 126, 127, 129, 132, 134, 137, 139, 141, 142, 145, 147, 148, 154, 160, 162, 167, 182, 188, 191, 203, 204
David Arragon, 54
DAVIDSON: Anne, 107
Davis: Elizabeth, 127
DAVIS: Alexander, 113; Charles, 56, 58; Fanny, 112; Griffith, 56; Henry, 112; Hugh, 112; Isaac, 128; Joshua, 112; Judith, 113, 115, 121, 132; Lucy, 83, 91; Lydia, 56; Marian, 113; Mary, 128; Matthew, 85; Melinda, 113; Redman, 112; Thomas, 83; William, 56, 112, 117, 127, 128
Davy, 11, 15, 19, 35, 38, 48, 66, 88, 95, 99, 108, 109, 111, 112, 114, 132, 138, 144, 146, 147, 151, 161, 165, 167, 168, 173, 174, 178, 184, 190, 194, 198, 201
DAY: Cassandra, 126; Cossom, 122, 126, 138; Francis, 126; Horatio, 126; Jemima, 126; John, 126; Paul W., 126; Susan, 126
Deale, 59
DEAN: Benjamin, 134
DEARING: Elias, 194
DeBARR: George, 90; John, 90
Deborah, 21
Decia, 10
DEGGETT: Benjamin, 18
Delah, 107
Delfa, 154
Delia, 62, 112, 128, 145, 147, 179, 183

13

Deliah, 81, 182
Delila, 61, 116
Delilah, 145, 146, 148, 155, 163, 166, 173, 174, 179, 190
Della, 133
Dellah, 97
Delph, 83
Delphe, 196
Delphia, 59, 63, 81, 82, 102, 130, 157
Delphina, 57, 153
Delphy, 109, 159, 161, 192
Delsey, 207
Dembo, 20, 30, 94, 98, 104, 113, 130
Demby, 22, 142
DENEALE: George, 97
Dennis, 59, 64, 74, 92, 102, 105, 118, 124, 127, 133, 137, 140, 143, 146, 151, 156, 158, 160, 181, 195
DENT: Eliza, 75; George, 74; Jennett, 75; William, 98
DEWLIN: John, 141
Diana, 108, 112, 141, 149, 158
Dianh, 194
Dianna, 129, 188
DIBILL: William, 152
Dick, 2, 3, 4, 5, 9, 10, 11, 16, 17, 18, 19, 20, 28, 29, 32, 34, 41, 42, 43, 44, 45, 46, 47, 49, 50, 53, 56, 57, 62, 63, 65, 67, 68, 72, 73, 74, 75, 76, 77, 79, 80, 87, 88, 93, 95, 100, 102, 103, 105, 108, 111, 114, 116, 117, 118, 122, 133, 134, 137, 139, 140, 141, 142, 144, 153, 156, 159, 163, 167, 170, 171, 174, 193, 194, 195, 201
Dick Jr., 105
Dick Sr., 105
DICKEY: Elizabeth, 170
Dicy, 107
Diddy, 4, 12, 14

DIGGS: Edward, 144; Elizabeth, 49, 144; Ludwell, 144; Porcia, 144; Sarah Duttley, 144; Thomas G., 144; Whiting, 106, 114, 115, 144; William Harry, 144
Dilcy, 204
Diley, 144
Dill, 61, 208
Dillir, 79
Dilly, 77, 82, 98
Dilsey, 207
Dimby, 8, 57
Dinah, 2, 11, 17, 18, 19, 20, 22, 27, 28, 29, 32, 33, 36, 38, 39, 42, 43, 44, 45, 50, 54, 55, 62, 64, 65, 66, 67, 68, 69, 73, 75, 77, 82, 94, 102, 103, 105, 110, 116, 122, 123, 124, 125, 126, 128, 131, 133, 134, 135, 137, 139, 145, 146, 147, 150, 159, 162, 163, 179, 181, 184, 194, 195, 196, 202, 203, 208
Diner, 51, 63, 64, 112, 125, 133, 144, 162
Dinia, 29
DIXON: Alex, 171, 196; Alexander, 187; Alice, 196, 205; Charles, 187, 196; Charles C., 171; Edward, 168, 186, 199; George B, 186, 199; George B., 167, 168; John, 187, 196; Lucius, 171, 187, 196; Maria, 167, 187, 196, 200, 205; Mary Jane, 168; Turner, 153, 168, 186, 191, 199; William, 196, 205
Diza, 120
DOBEY: James, 67, 77
DOBSON: Enoch, 14
Doctor, 17
DODD: Allen, 28; Ann, 119, 187; Benjamin, 28, 77, 123, 128, 198; Eleanor, 146, 187;

Elenor, 119; Elizabeth, 123; George, 141; Hester, 56; James, 28, 119, 187; John, 28, 119, 128, 146, 187; Joseph, 119, 187; Joseph R, 200; Levi, 159; Mahethalem, 119, 146; Mehithelem, 187; Nathaniel, 28, 29, 77, 118, 119, 145, 146, 166, 187; Sanford, 187; Sarah, 28, 69, 77, 82; Travis, 123

DODSON: Abraham, 5; Barbary, 5; Enoch, 5; Greenham, 14, 27; Molly, 5; Tabitha, 5

Dole, 37

DOLEY: Ann, 73

Doll, 4, 9, 23, 36, 37, 42, 74, 117

Dolly, 58, 59, 79, 81, 104, 117, 121, 130, 142, 168, 175, 190, 191, 199

Domina, 9

Domini, 190

Donathan, 195

DONIDALL: Bowmer, 124

DOORES: Edgar, 208

Doras Kitty, 12

Dorcas, 16, 31, 86, 87, 188

Dorcus, 9, 10, 30, 53, 80, 128

Dorkas, 31, 32

Dorvell, 117

Dosha, 116

DOUGHTY: Helen, 207

Douglas, 62

Dover, 4

DOWELL: Elisha, 76; Elizabeth, 76; Nehemiah, 76, 87

DOWELL Sr.: Nehemiah, 93

Dowing, 143

DOWNS: Henry, 185

DRUMMOND: Suckey, 15

Drusilla, 194, 195

Dublin, 10, 11, 13, 37, 200

DUFF: Nathaniel, 197

DUGARD: Doc. John, 16

Duke, 41

Dulin, 34

DULIN: George, 64; William, 64, 65; William Eelzey, 64

Dully, 177

DUNCAN: Anne, 142; Charles, 85, 134, 142, 146, 151; Dillard, 151; Edmund, 151; Elias, 50; Housen, 42, 52; Howson, 56; Joseph, 42, 43, 52, 56, 103; Letitia, 207; Lettice, 191; Lidya, 42; Lucinda, 50; Lyddia, 52, 53; Lydia, 57; Mariah, 142; Miriah, 151; Mrs, 151; Mrs. Dillard, 170; Nanny, 27; Samuel, 28; Travis, 151; Willis, 50

DUNCAN Sr.: John, 50

Dyner, 120, 132

Eady, 99, 124, 129

Easter, 9, 32, 44, 53, 54, 56, 58, 60, 64, 68, 69, 71, 80, 82, 86, 93, 105, 130, 146, 164, 184, 185, 192

EASTHAM: Bird, 197; George, 197; John, 197

Easty, 40

Eda, 185

Edda, 137

Eddee, 90

EDDINGTON: William, 158

Eddy, 143

Ede, 148

Edenborough, 109

EDGE: Fossicar, 139

Edia, 70

Edie, 92, 104, 163, 188

Edith, 150

Edmond, 36, 40, 41, 46, 49, 54, 68, 69, 83, 102, 110, 112, 116, 123, 129, 131, 133, 138,

15

141, 146, 151, 155, 159, 165, 166, 170, 173, 183, 194, 195, 200, 206

EDMOND: Nancy E., 107; Thomas W., 107

EDMONDS: Anne, 6; Betty, 6; Col. Elias, 64; Col. William, 59; Elias, 6, 72, 111, 127, 130, 169; Elizabeth, 131; George, 72; Helen, 72; James, 130; John, 58, 72, 130; Judith, 6; Peggy, 72; Sarah, 131, 135; Sarah B., 127, 140; William, 72, 130, 133, 163, 169; William Foote, 163

Edmund, 66, 68, 83, 85, 109, 121, 124, 126, 127, 128, 132, 134, 160, 162, 170, 173, 174, 178, 180, 181, 183, 198, 206

Edmund Jr., 170

Edmund M, 178

EDRINGTON: John, 7

Edward, 51, 67, 80, 124, 158, 162, 169, 186, 192, 199, 204

EDWARD: John, 127

Edwin, 200

Edy, 66, 103, 113, 127, 137, 149, 153, 180, 205

Effy, 34

Eglantine, 160

Egwood, 166

Eide, 32

Eleanor, 8, 113, 128, 143, 160

Elender, 74, 101, 192

Elgin, 20, 191

Eli, 2, 116, 155, 158, 168, 173, 174, 175, 193

Elias, 32, 65, 75, 77, 84, 92, 101, 104, 117, 119, 120, 124, 132, 154, 159, 163, 165, 166, 168, 170, 174, 175, 177, 187, 190, 194, 196, 198, 200, 201, 206

Elijah, 43, 46, 56, 67, 74, 79, 90, 101, 109, 118, 128, 137, 140, 160, 162, 164, 165, 170, 189, 206

Elisa, 103, 146, 154, 162, 172, 187

Elisha, 162

Elisha Briggs, 1, 4

Eliza, 40, 45, 61, 62, 81, 87, 91, 104, 105, 109, 112, 116, 118, 119, 120, 121, 123, 124, 125, 126, 127, 129, 134, 137, 139, 141, 147, 149, 152, 154, 155, 156, 160, 164, 167, 170, 174, 178, 183, 187, 188, 191, 192, 193, 194, 195, 196, 202, 203, 204, 205, 206, 207

Elizabeth, 27, 31, 94, 131, 133, 141, 154, 159, 188, 194, 195, 200, 201, 207

Elizabeth Davis, 127

ELKIN: David, 139; Philip, 139

Ell, 38, 121

Ellen, 174, 193, 194, 203, 205, 206

ELLESS: John, 171; Nathan, 171

Ellick, 64, 72, 116, 153, 194

ELLIOTT: John, 37; Reuben, 20; Thomas, 20

Ellis, 62, 168

ELLIS: Betsy, 120; James, 120, 121; Nathan, 167

Elsie, 17, 55, 58, 199

Ely, 1, 147

Elymus, 30

Emancipated: Aaron, 66; Abraham, 178; Alla, 115; Aminta, 33; Betty, 115; Billy, 64; Bob, 45, 64; Celah, 69; Charles, 163; Charlotte Grace, 97; Chloe, 125; Diner, 125; Dorcus, 9; Embry, 69; Fanny, 163; Gloster, 66; Hannah, 125,

16

134; Harry, 64; Jack, 134; Jane, 66; John, 41, 125; Joseph, 178; Martin, 45; Melinda, 202; Molly, 64; Moses, 64; Roger, 45; Sally, 64; Sam, 64; Scipio, 64; Sookey, 178; Sucky, 64; Tom, 64; Venus, 66; Washington, 115; William, 125; Winny, 64

Emanuel, 54, 66, 79, 93, 94, 98, 109, 110, 114, 137, 179, 197, 201

Ember, 46

EMBREY: Albert G., 123; John, 126; John Thompson, 123; Mary, 144; Robert, 123, 127; Walker, 123

EMBREY Jr.: William, 144

EMBREY Sr.: William, 144

Embry, 69

EMBRY: George, 99; William, 189, 194, 199

Emila, 104, 167

Emily, 122, 124, 129, 144, 145, 146, 148, 150, 151, 173, 174, 192, 195, 197, 200, 201, 202, 208

Emma, 160, 162, 174, 187, 193

Emmanuel, 141

Emmeline, 205

EMMONS: Ann, 156; William, 50, 51

Emmy, 141

Emsy, 122, 146

ENGLISH: Betsey, 90; Betsy, 111, 150; Frosty, 111; Icy, 111; James, 90, 111; Jerry, 150; John, 90, 111; Joseph, 88, 90, 111, 150; Joy, 90; Margaret, 90; Polly, 90; Robert, 86; Sarah, 205; Thornton, 90; William, 90, 111; Zephiriah, 150

Enis, 128

Ennis, 31, 117, 151

Enoch, 74, 82, 103, 117, 160, 167, 174, 194, 203

ENSOR: Eleanor, 110; George, 102, 110; James, 110; Jemimah, 103; Mary, 110; Stephen, 110; Thomas, 110

ENSOR Jr.: William R., 110

Ephraim, 16, 51, 54, 81, 82, 88, 90, 98, 108, 111, 112, 115, 123, 149, 151, 153, 157, 164, 166

Erasmus, 115

Eredocia, 10

Eridocia, 11, 13

Esau, 81, 103, 186

ESKRIDGE: John, 145; Samuel, 17; Sarah, 207

ESKRIDGE alias KENNER: Samuel, 17

Essea, 82

Essex, 188

Estate of Vermont (DIXON), 171, 205

Ester, 11, 106, 151

Esther, 1, 10, 11, 13, 17, 18, 20, 23, 27, 30, 41, 44, 45, 59, 60, 62, 66, 81, 105, 117, 123, 128, 138, 153, 155, 159, 178, 200

Ethen, 116

ETHERINGTON: Elizabeth, 15, 16; John, 6

Eugene, 38, 53

Eury, 196, 204

EUSTACE: Anne, 63; Eliza, 121; Hancock, 63, 142; Mary, 39, 63; William, 39, 63, 64, 142, 160, 204

Eva, 18

Evan, 12, 21

EVANS: Elisha, 156; Martha, 30; Richard, 129

Eve, 32, 33, 41, 47, 64, 65, 103, 104, 107, 111, 139, 143, 160, 180
Evelina, 84, 102, 143, 153, 167, 177, 178, 194, 207
Eveline, 88, 101, 178, 192, 207
EWELE: Elizabeth, 86
Ezchiel, 169
Ezekial, 111, 170
Ezekiel, 20, 62, 69

Famar, 194
Fan, 60, 66, 68, 72, 75, 77, 80, 90
Fander, 140
Fann, 44
Fanna, 101, 105
Fanny, 17, 46, 49, 50, 54, 59, 60, 64, 65, 66, 67, 68, 70, 71, 72, 73, 77, 78, 81, 83, 84, 85, 86, 88, 99, 100, 101, 102, 108, 109, 111, 112, 113, 114, 115, 116, 117, 120, 122, 124, 127, 128, 132, 138, 141, 143, 144, 148, 150, 153, 155, 156, 157, 158, 160, 161, 163, 165, 166, 170, 172, 173, 174, 175, 179, 181, 185, 187, 188, 190, 192, 193, 196, 200, 202, 203, 204, 207, 208
FANT: Nancy, 132
Fara, 103
FARGANSON: Molly, 39
Farne, 85
Farrow, 179
FARROW: B., 81; Benjamin, 39; Capt. George, 91, 94; Lucy, 108; Nimrod, 112
Faulton, 90
Faun, 90
Fay, 109
FEAGAN: Edward, 54, 149; Gracy, 155
FEAGIN: Edward, 19; Elizabeth, 19

Federick, 169
Felicia, 16, 111, 121, 160, 169, 178, 186, 205
Fellows, 64
Fender, 52, 53
Fenton, 163, 195
FICKLIN: Anthony L., 132; Anthony Strother, 131; Betsy, 132; Charles, 131; Charles B., 132; Drucella Nancy Harriet, 132; Maria P., 132; Mary, 131; Susan B., 132
FICKLIN Jr.: Charles B., 138
FICKLIN Sr.: Charles B., 138
FIELD: Daniel, 23, 24; Fielden, 23; George, 23; Hannah, 204; John, 23; Lewis, 23; Sarah, 24
Fielding, 51, 54, 59, 124, 133, 188, 202, 208
FIELDING: Edward, 28; Edwin, 27; Nancy, 27
Fill, 46
FISHBACK: Ann, 71; Jacob, 1; Jesse, 71; John, 35, 71, 82; Joseph, 71; Josiah, 58, 71; Philip, 150, 178; Phillip, 200
FISHER: Dunlap, 85; Thomas, 106
Fitzallen, 195
FITZHUGH: Battaile, 135, 140; Cole, 140; Dudley, 140; George, 166; Henry, 166; Ludwell, 140; Thomas, 166; William, 135, 137, 140, 150; William D., 135
Flander, 125
Flemin, 110
Fleming, 165, 192
FLETCHER: Agness, 108; John, 111; Joshua, 108, 110, 159
Flo, 36

Flora, 58, 72, 77, 80, 122, 123, 127, 193, 194, 195, 202

Flors, 75

FLOWERREE: Catherine A., 175; Charlotte, 132; Daniel, 120, 132, 175; French, 132, 158, 162, 173, 177, 199; John, 129, 132; Joseph F., 175; Joseph L., 175; Kemp, 98, 100; Margaret, 132; Sally, 132; Susan M., 175; William, 117, 132, 154; William K., 175

FOLEY: Bayliss, 190; Bryant, 109, 163; Capt James, 192; Catherine, 207; Cecilia, 185; Elizabeth, 52; Enoch, 127, 129; James, 52, 54, 130, 191, 203; John, 129; Kitty, 191; Lettice, 52; Mary, 47; Molly, 52; Sally, 191; Sarah, 10; Thomas, 191, 207; William, 129, 190

FOOTE: Behethelon, 1; Celia, 13, 33; Elizabeth, 1; Frances, 1; George, 1, 2, 5, 13, 16; George William, 163; Gibson, 6; Gilson, 1; Henry, 1; Hesther, 13; Mary, 1; Richard, 1, 9; Richard Helen, 13; William, 1, 9; William Richard, 3

Forrester, 5, 14, 27

Fortune, 17, 51, 87

FOSTER: Priscilla, 98

Fountaina, 160

FOUSHEE: Polly, 132

FOWKE: Ann Harrison, 10; Chandler, 21; Elizabeth, 21, 22; Enfield, 21; George, 21; Gerand, 21; Mary, 10, 21; Robert, 21; Thomas Harrison, 10; William, 21

FOWLER: William, 32, 92, 100

FOX: Elizabeth, 97, 98; James, 80, 82, 98; John, 80, 83, 98, 206; Samuel, 67, 80, 81, 82

Fran, 90

Frances, 80, 87, 92, 166, 185, 197, 201

Francis, 11, 20, 22, 54, 60, 61, 79, 94, 117, 142, 143, 166, 207

Frank, 1, 2, 3, 4, 7, 10, 11, 13, 14, 16, 17, 20, 21, 22, 23, 24, 28, 33, 34, 36, 38, 39, 42, 46, 49, 51, 52, 53, 54, 57, 58, 59, 60, 62, 65, 66, 67, 68, 72, 73, 74, 88, 97, 101, 102, 104, 108, 109, 113, 114, 119, 121, 122, 124, 129, 130, 133, 137, 140, 153, 154, 159, 160, 162, 163, 165, 166, 175, 178, 182, 193, 195, 196, 199

Frank Lage, 10

FRANKLIN: Lucy Jackson, 144; Margaret, 144; Thomas Albert, 144; William, 144, 150; William Edward, 144

Franky, 66, 73, 80, 88, 103, 105, 143, 154, 159, 163, 174, 178, 192

Franny, 88

Frederic, 116

Frederich, 111, 142, 192

Frederick, 39, 40, 68, 81, 82, 88, 123, 146, 147, 160, 163, 167, 174, 179, 182, 189, 192, 193, 195, 200, 203

Fredrick, 90

FREEMAN: Elizabeth, 161; Garrett, 40, 208; James, 40, 119; Lail, 180; Nathaniel, 40, 208; Sally, 197, 208; Stephen, 208; Thomas, 180; William, 24, 36; William C, 197, 202, 208

FRENCH: Elizabeth, 94, 104; John, 88; Reuben, 188

FURGESON: Mary, 130
FURR: Charles, 90; Enoch, 102; Frances, 89; Minor, 91; W., 92; William Charles, 89

Gabe, 194
Gabriel, 36, 38, 41, 44, 52, 53, 59, 60, 72, 73, 84, 88, 101, 105, 114, 120, 124, 127, 133, 137, 150, 155, 167, 174, 188, 189, 190, 192, 193, 194, 195, 200, 203, 205
Gabriel Jr., 133
GAINER: Benjamin, 37
GAINS: Elizabeth, 161
GAMER: Susan, 162
Gancelos, 4
Gandison, 194
Garland, 62
GARNER: Charles, 55; James, 86, 90; John, 3; Vincent, 49, 63, 75, 181, 191; William W, 191
Garrison, 120, 132
GARRISON: Nehemiah, 126
GAUNT: John, 121, 127, 133
Gelberd, 79
Gen, 6, 14
General, 174, 193
Gensy, 6
George, 2, 4, 6, 7, 8, 9, 10, 13, 15, 17, 18, 20, 21, 22, 24, 27, 28, 29, 30, 31, 32, 35, 36, 37, 38, 39, 40, 41, 42, 44, 46, 50, 51, 52, 53, 54, 55, 56, 57, 58, 59, 61, 62, 63, 64, 65, 66, 67, 68, 69, 71, 72, 73, 74, 75, 76, 78, 79, 80, 81, 82, 84, 85, 86, 87, 88, 89, 91, 93, 94, 95, 98, 99, 100, 101, 102, 103, 104, 105, 106, 107, 108, 110, 112, 113, 114, 116, 117, 118, 119, 122, 123, 124, 125, 126, 127, 128, 129, 131, 133, 134, 135, 137, 138, 139, 140, 141, 142,

143, 144, 145, 147, 148, 149, 150, 151, 153, 154, 155, 156, 157, 158, 159, 160, 162, 164, 165, 166, 167, 169, 170, 172, 173, 174, 177, 178, 180, 183, 185, 188, 189, 191, 192, 193, 194, 195, 198, 200, 202, 203, 204, 206, 208
GEORGE: Aaron, 39; Abner, 54; Capt. Nicholas, 19; Cumberland, 134; Fanny, 54; Joseph, 121, 122, 134, 156; Nicholas, 18; Parnack, 51, 54; Peggy, 54; Reuben, 54; William, 134, 156; Wilmoth, 54
George Jr, 103, 207
Gerand, 36, 180
Gerard, 23, 27, 37, 66, 89, 91, 93, 111, 120, 125, 127, 149, 165, 167, 169, 174, 179, 188, 195, 196
Gertrude, 195
Geu, 85
Gib, 128
Gibbans, 144
Gibson, 142
GIBSON: Abraham, 64; Ann Grayson, 10; Benjamin H., 160; Betsy, 117; George, 93, 94; James, 145; John, 10, 38, 142; Jonathan, 38, 48, 53, 60; Jonathan Catlett, 10; Jonathan Cattlett, 38; Margaret, 143; Margaret Cattlett, 38; Mary, 38, 94; Moses, 126, 182; Sally, 117; Susanna Grayson, 38; Susannah, 10; Thomas, 9, 10, 38; William, 112, 117, 119, 126, 182
Gilbert, 74, 111, 112, 128, 179, 194, 207
Giles, 204
Gill, 203, 207

Gilla, 32
GILLISON: Ann, 10; James, 39, 69; Jno., 178; John, 10, 39, 182, 186
GILLISON Sr.: James, 58
GILSON: John, 63; Thomas, 73
Gin, 103
Gin Amanda, 102
Ginn, 3, 116
Ginny, 144, 145, 149, 150, 163, 205
GLANVILLE: Thomas, 114, 115
Glascock, 133
GLASCOCK, 84; Addison, 191, 198; Aguila, 189; Alex, 161; Archibald, 161; Benjamin, 132; Climina, 64; Daniel, 145; Frances, 151, 152, 177; French, 143, 145; George, 189, 191; Gregory, 161; Hannah, 189; Hezekiah, 143, 144, 145, 147; Irael, 161; Israel, 151; James, 145; Jesse, 188; John, 55, 71, 143, 145; Nancy, 143; Polly, 143, 145; Sarah, 143; Susanna, 143; Thomas, 84, 106, 162, 205, 208; William, 161
Glascon, 127
Glasgow, 19
Glassco, 46
GLASSCOCK: Agatha, 43; John, 28; Thomas, 43
Glasson, 121
GLENDENINGS: Rosanna, 124
GLENDENNY: Betsy, 62
Gloster, 54, 66, 109
Gloucester, 28, 68
Godfrey, 16, 155
Goen, 208
GOLDIN: Thornton, 187
GORDON: B, 190; Elizabeth, 135; Francis, 106; John, 75,

106; Peggy, 106; Sarah, 188; Thomas, 95, 106; William, 106
GORE: Mary, 154, 162
Gowin, 131, 138
Grace, 10, 11, 12, 22, 31, 39, 43, 45, 56, 57, 58, 61, 62, 64, 65, 66, 69, 71, 72, 84, 85, 88, 94, 100, 102, 103, 104, 105, 111, 113, 118, 121, 125, 128, 131, 137, 140, 143, 144, 145, 146, 147, 150, 155, 156, 158, 160, 162, 167, 168, 170, 174, 181, 182, 193, 195, 197
Gracie, 29
GRAHAM: Celia, 43; Duncan, 58, 61, 69, 86; Eva, 152; Mrs., 17; Nancy, 69; Peter, 152, 179, 181; William, 69
Granderson, 162
Grandison, 124, 184
GRANT: Peter, 99, 121; Susanna, 125; Susannar, 16
Grason, 195
GRAY: Bennedicton, 101; Henry H., 101; Samuel, 83, 89, 101
Great Will, 52
GREEN: Charles, 148, 171; Duff, 4; Elizabeth, 157; Frankey, 130; George, 92, 101; James, 121; John, 170; Joseph, 121, 122; Lucy, 131; Mary A, 199; Mary A., 171; Robert, 170, 181; William, 81
Griffin, 15, 18, 95, 177
GRIFFIN: Helen, 55
GRIFFITH: Dennis, 147, 158, 191; Evan, 50
GRIGBY: Capt. William, 23
GRIGSBY, 57; Bayless, 44, 180; Elizabeth, 203; Enoch, 70; John, 7, 35, 37, 44; Lewis, 44, 132; Nathaniel,

132; Samuel, 21, 22; Taliaferro, 102
GRIMSLEY: William, 151
GUNNELL: Ann, 145; James, 145, 147, 179, 181
Gus, 88, 89, 101, 206
Gust, 99
Gusta, 129
Gustavus, 194
Gut Wi__e, 152
GUTRIDGE: Elizabeth, 199; John F, 187
Guy, 17, 27, 50

HACHLEY: Francis, 62; Jael, 62; Lot, 62
Hagar, 33, 44, 46, 68, 76, 111, 112, 122, 126, 133, 169
Hagga, 29
Hailey, 108
HAILEY: John, 79, 163; Joseph, 163
HALE: Frances P., 140; Francis T., 140; George, 87, 140; Henry D., 140; John, 90; Margaret P., 140; William, 140, 143, 195
HALEY: John, 35
HALL: Richard, 4, 12, 14; Richard Lingan, 14
HALLEY: James M, 190
HAMBLETON: William, 35, 37
Hamer, 12
HAMILTON: Euphame, 155, 156; Henry, 34, 63; William, 34, 35, 37
Hamitt, 61
Hampshier, 39
HAMPTON: Ann, 165, 173; Anne, 177; Elizabeth, 4; Fanny, 98; Gale, 4; Jno., 200; John, 192, 205; Joseph, 71, 75, 97, 118; Martha, 4; Mary, 36, 106; Richard, 4;

Sarah, 4; Sarah Lucelia, 203; Susanna, 11; William H, 198; William H., 165, 177
HANDEY: Eve, 202, 203, 207
Haney, 98
Hanna, 163
Hannah, 2, 6, 7, 8, 9, 10, 11, 12, 13, 15, 16, 17, 18, 19, 20, 21, 22, 27, 29, 30, 31, 32, 33, 34, 35, 36, 37, 38, 40, 42, 43, 45, 47, 49, 50, 51, 52, 54, 55, 58, 59, 60, 61, 62, 63, 64, 65, 66, 67, 68, 70, 71, 72, 73, 74, 76, 78, 80, 84, 87, 88, 89, 91, 93, 95, 97, 98, 99, 101, 103, 104, 107, 108, 109, 110, 111, 112, 113, 116, 117, 118, 119, 120, 121, 122, 123, 124, 125, 126, 127, 129, 130, 132, 134, 137, 138, 139, 140, 141, 143, 146, 148, 149, 150, 151, 153, 154, 155, 156, 158, 159, 160, 161, 162, 163, 164, 165, 166, 169, 171, 172, 173, 174, 177, 180, 181, 182, 183, 184, 185, 186, 188, 189, 192, 194, 195, 196, 205, 206
Hannah Janny, 86
Hannah Sr., 80
Hanner, 16, 35, 79, 88, 100, 104, 108, 112, 131, 134, 147, 158, 167, 200
Hannibal, 58, 72, 89, 108, 109, 114, 144, 145
HANSBERRY: Gabriel, 62
HANSFORD: Alexander, 98, 100
Hanson, 104
HANSON: Ann, 68
Hany, 57
Har_, 53
Hardy, 188
Harlow, 75, 93
Harriet, 35, 49, 65, 68, 70, 72, 73, 78, 79, 93, 100, 101, 102,

104, 105, 108, 114, 116, 117,
119, 121, 123, 124, 127, 128,
129, 133, 137, 140, 143, 147,
151, 154, 155, 158, 159, 162,
163, 164, 165, 166, 167, 168,
170, 172, 173, 174, 175, 178,
179, 181, 184, 188, 192, 193,
194, 195, 196, 198, 201, 202,
207
Harris, 160, 161
HARRIS: Thomas, 192
Harrison, 53, 74, 79, 129, 154,
158, 160, 181, 185, 196, 204
HARRISON: Benjamin, 9, 10,
54, 55, 62, 77; Burr, 10, 37,
41, 154, 156, 165; George P,
204; Jane, 41; Lucy, 10, 41;
Thomas, 9, 10, 11; Thomas
G, 204; William, 10, 13, 204
HARRISON Jr: William, 37
Harry, 2, 4, 5, 6, 7, 9, 10, 11,
15, 16, 20, 23, 27, 28, 31, 32,
34, 35, 36, 37, 38, 40, 42, 43,
44, 45, 46, 47, 49, 50, 52, 53,
54, 57, 58, 59, 60, 61, 62, 63,
64, 67, 68, 70, 71, 72, 73, 74,
75, 76, 77, 78, 79, 80, 84, 86,
87, 88, 91, 93, 94, 97, 98,
103, 105, 108, 114, 116, 117,
119, 121, 122, 123, 124, 125,
126, 128, 129, 130, 131, 132,
134, 138, 141, 144, 148, 149,
150, 151, 152, 153, 154, 155,
156, 158, 160, 161, 162, 163,
164, 165, 168, 169, 173, 174,
178, 180, 181, 184, 189, 190,
191, 192, 194, 200, 201, 202,
204, 205, 208
Harry Dade, 192
Harry Jr., 133
Harry Shafford, 36
HARSBROUGH: William, 8
HART: Catherine, 126; Robert,
134
Hartley, 149

HARVEY: Richard, 82
Hasse, 180
Hath, 19
HATHAWAY: Capt. John, 33;
Elizabeth, 33; Francis I.,
135; James, 59; Joanna, 11;
John, 33, 57, 106; Sarah, 33
Hattimah, 21
Haunton, 114, 128
HAWKINS: Alice C., 138;
John, 71
Hay, 109
HEADLEY: James, 42
HEALE: George, 86
HEALY: John, 34; Mary, 34;
William, 34
Heath, 31, 42
Hector, 190
Heffy, 27
Heflin, 171
Helen, 77, 86, 101, 102, 112,
158, 190, 201
HELM: Betsy, 124; Elizabeth,
155; Letty, 11; Thomas, 39
HELME: Agga, 119; Lucy, 119
Hembum, 162
Henders: Henry, 15; John, 15
Henderson, 57, 125
HENESTREET: James, 153
Heney, 180
Henley, 60, 61
Henny, 53, 90, 92, 99, 102, 142,
144, 145, 149, 196
Henrietta, 188
Henry, 2, 3, 16, 17, 20, 22, 30,
31, 39, 42, 48, 52, 54, 56, 57,
59, 66, 68, 69, 73, 74, 80, 81,
84, 88, 89, 90, 91, 94, 95, 97,
101, 102, 108, 110, 111, 112,
113, 114, 115, 116, 118, 119,
122, 123, 126, 128, 131, 137,
138, 139, 143, 145, 146, 148,
153, 154, 155, 156, 157, 158,
160, 162, 164, 167, 169, 170,
172, 173, 174, 177, 178, 179,

181, 183, 188, 189, 190, 194, 195, 198, 200, 201, 202, 203, 204, 206, 207
Henry Henders, 15
Henry Jr, 181
Henson, 61, 88
Hercules, 4
HEREFORD: Francis, 198, 202
HERNDON: Alvin, 85; John, 85, 134; John C., 85; Traverse, 85
HERNDOW: John, 83
Hester, 22, 57, 59, 87, 111, 169, 201, 203
Heth, 127, 170
Hethe, 49
Hetheliah, 32
Hethey, 21, 28, 43, 53
Hetty, 125, 139, 156
Hezekiah, 11, 12
HICKERSON: Daniel, 134; John, 66; Joseph, 122, 127
HICKS: Stephen, 168
Hill, 188
Hilly, 200
HINKERSON: Abraham, 195
HINSON: James, 66; Robert, 66, 67; Taply, 66
Hiram, 151, 152, 159, 160, 177, 179, 191, 198, 203
HITCH: Aguilla, 127, 201; Cassandra, 201; Cassey, 82; Christopher, 85; Freeman, 120; John, 68, 82; Mary, 201; Nathan, 74, 82, 85, 107, 142; Tilman, 160, 161; Truman, 82
Hith, 111
HITT: Alice Katharine, 1; Benjamin, 148; Franky, 44; Harmon, 8; Joel, 103; John, 8, 24, 82; Mary, 2; Nimrod, 103; Peter, 8, 75, 144, 150, 151; Reuben, 103
HITT Jr.: Peter, 151

HITT Sr.: Peter, 103
Holland, 18, 19
HOLMES: Willis, 153
HOLTZCLAW: Archabald, 103; Archibald, 44; Catherine, 44; Eli, 44; Harman, 1; Henry, 1; Jacob, 1, 2; Jno, 164; John, 183; Joseph, 1, 32, 44; Josiah, 130; Milly, 5; Sally, 44; Stephen, 44
HOMER: Frances, 73; Gustavus B., 73
HOMES: Diadima, 83; Edmond, 83; Gustavus B., 128; James, 83; Nathaniel, 99
HOOD: Fanny, 148; Francis, 141; George, 134, 164; John, 141; Robert Houson, 141
HOOMES: Edmund, 90; Edward, 102
HOORE: George, 134
Hoping John, 42
HOPKINS: David, 63, 79
Horace, 78, 130, 141, 160, 185
HORD: Agatha, 163, 167, 189; Ambrose, 167; Ann Scott, 175; Charity, 161, 167; Enos, 167; Frances, 169; James, 163, 167, 174, 189; Margrit, 163; Peggy, 161; Thomas, 163; William, 161, 167
HORNER: Doc. Gustavus B., 68, 143, 148; Federick, 198; Frederick, 189; G B, 198; G.B., 157; Gustavus B., 120, 156; John, 68; Mary, 131; William, 68
HORTON: Enoch, 159; Thomas, 166
HOUGHTON: Cadwallader, 32
HOVE: John, 150, 184
Howard, 103, 124, 127

HUDNALL, 178; Frances, 110; Francis, 207; John, 103; Nancy, 110
HUDSON: Dennis, 77
Hugh, 7, 75, 106
HUGHES: Catherine, 130; Margaret Downing, 108; Thomas, 109
Hulda, 69, 76, 194, 203
Hulder, 127
Huldy, 207
HUME: Asa, 107; Caty, 196; Daniel Bradford, 116; Eliza, 116; Enoch, 107; George, 102, 196; Jacob, 107; Jenny, 107; Katy, 116; Margaret, 116, 132; McKay, 107, 132; Peggy, 107; Robert, 102, 107; Sarah, 107, 132
Humphrey, 53, 66, 68, 178, 179
HUMPHRIS: Lucinda, 107
HUMSTEAD: Susannah, 9
HUNT: Samuel, 60
Hunter, 74, 79
HUNTER: Thomas L., 177
Hunton, 107
HUNTON: Catherine, 125; Gen Thomas, 194; James, 98, 170, 180; John, 101; Mary, 51; T L, 187; Thomas, 98; Thomas Edward, 203; William, 98, 99, 170; William W., 133

Idea, 117
Immanuel, 9, 67, 81
INGRAM: Lucy, 106, 114, 115; Thomas, 78, 114, 115
Inman, 192
Irene, 56
Iride, 191
Isaac, 10, 11, 13, 16, 17, 21, 25, 27, 28, 38, 49, 52, 53, 61, 62, 71, 80, 81, 82, 92, 103, 106, 111, 112, 133, 138, 147, 153, 154, 159, 169, 172, 174, 178, 179, 180, 188, 192, 193, 194, 199, 200, 203, 204, 206, 207
Isaac Jr., 175
Isabell, 68, 81, 83, 108, 109, 114, 159, 180, 188
Isabella, 3, 129, 130, 139, 159
Isham, 162
Israel, 147
Ivy, 56
Izza, 42

Jaby, 130
Jack, 1, 2, 3, 4, 5, 6, 7, 8, 9, 10, 11, 12, 14, 15, 18, 20, 22, 23, 24, 28, 29, 31, 33, 34, 35, 37, 38, 43, 44, 45, 50, 51, 52, 53, 56, 57, 58, 59, 61, 62, 63, 64, 67, 68, 69, 70, 71, 73, 75, 76, 77, 79, 80, 81, 83, 84, 85, 87, 88, 91, 98, 99, 101, 102, 103, 104, 105, 107, 108, 110, 112, 113, 114, 117, 118, 120, 121, 122, 123, 124, 125, 126, 127, 128, 129, 130, 132, 134, 139, 141, 143, 145, 153, 156, 158, 159, 162, 164, 165, 166, 167, 170, 172, 173, 174, 178, 179, 180, 183, 188, 193, 194, 195, 203, 206, 208
Jack Clary, 60
Jack Fox, 108
Jack Grace, 99
Jack Jr., 80
Jack Kent, 20
Jack Monday, 16, 18
JACKMAN: Hannah, 58; John, 22; Joseph, 22; Thomas, 22, 60; William, 22
Jackson, 133, 181, 201, 204
JACKSON: Magdelen, 8
Jackwood, 87, 91
Jacky, 9
Jacob, 10, 11, 12, 16, 17, 23, 30, 32, 38, 42, 44, 45, 50, 52,

53, 54, 58, 60, 61, 62, 64, 65, 69, 70, 72, 73, 74, 79, 80, 81, 83, 84, 86, 87, 88, 91, 92, 97, 99, 103, 113, 122, 126, 139, 143, 158, 159, 161, 162, 169, 194, 196
Jacob Jr., 133
Jacob Sr., 133
JACOBS: David, 179
Jael, 29, 33, 82
Jaley, 155
Jam, 154
Jame, 178
James, 2, 4, 5, 6, 7, 8, 9, 10, 12, 13, 15, 16, 17, 18, 20, 22, 23, 28, 29, 31, 32, 33, 34, 35, 37, 38, 39, 40, 41, 42, 43, 45, 46, 49, 50, 51, 52, 53, 54, 55, 56, 57, 58, 60, 61, 62, 63, 64, 65, 66, 67, 68, 69, 70, 71, 72, 73, 74, 76, 77, 79, 80, 81, 82, 84, 85, 87, 90, 92, 93, 94, 98, 101, 102, 103, 104, 105, 108, 109, 110, 111, 112, 113, 114, 117, 118, 120, 123, 124, 129, 130, 133, 139, 141, 143, 149, 153, 154, 155, 156, 159, 160, 162, 166, 167, 169, 170, 172, 173, 178, 180, 183, 189, 190, 192, 194, 195, 196, 197, 200, 204, 206, 207, 208
JAMES: Aldridge, 108, 160; Benjamin, 16, 75, 79, 128, 129; Betsy, 108, 160; Capt. James, 20; David, 160, 161; George, 103, 104; John, 16, 20, 67, 71; Lester, 108; Margaret, 108, 160; Thomas, 18, 81
James Alexander, 38
James Betty, 130
James Currie, 108
James James, 14
James Mathas, 197
James S__te, 10, 11

James Westward, 185
Jameson, 162
Jamima, 60, 67, 159
Jamina, 150
Jammy, 54, 153
Jane, 1, 2, 3, 4, 5, 7, 8, 10, 15, 20, 21, 22, 24, 27, 29, 31, 35, 37, 39, 40, 43, 51, 52, 53, 56, 59, 63, 64, 65, 66, 67, 68, 70, 71, 73, 75, 76, 79, 80, 81, 82, 86, 94, 95, 98, 101, 102, 105, 106, 108, 110, 114, 116, 118, 119, 121, 123, 124, 126, 127, 128, 132, 134, 137, 140, 141, 142, 143, 147, 148, 149, 153, 156, 162, 164, 165, 166, 167, 170, 171, 179, 182, 186, 188, 191, 194, 195, 197, 202, 203, 205, 206
Janerpher, 8
Janet, 153
Janey, 33, 53
Janny, 31, 50, 73, 76, 99, 100, 127, 133, 137, 141, 148, 180
Jarrett, 76, 103, 153
Jarvis, 50, 67
Jasainiah, 154
Jasper, 196, 204
Jauney, 157
Jawney, 18
Jax, 145, 147, 179
Je___y, 61
Jean, 2, 3, 10, 16, 24, 30, 31, 41, 81, 146
Jeanna, 72
Jeanny, 32
Jeany, 2, 109
Jedd, 15
Jeffrey, 2, 10, 11, 29, 39, 69, 72, 74, 77, 82, 87, 104, 111, 118, 119, 124, 127, 142, 151, 169, 205, 206, 207
Jeffrey Lynn, 129
JEFFRIES: Aggy, 197; Agnes, 184; Alexander, 196;

Elizabeth, 44; Enoch, 196; George, 130; James, 148; John, 94, 95; Joseph, 92, 196; Mary, 39; William, 196

Jeffry, 2, 23

Jem, 34

Jemima, 20, 31, 32, 46, 56, 61, 63, 66, 68, 93, 97, 129, 181, 195

Jemimah, 170

Jemimy, 140, 181

Jemina, 19, 31, 124

Jeminah, 82

Jemmy, 13

Jen, 22

Jencey, 173, 174

Jenna, 11, 116

JENNINGS: Augustine, 16, 103, 124, 129; Baylor, 17, 51; Berryman, 16, 23, 25; Elizabeth, 103; George, 17, 36; Hannah, 16, 17; John, 124; Lewis, 17, 103; Molly, 124; Sally, 17; Susanna, 25; Thomas O, 208; Thomas O., 124; William, 16, 28, 103; William H., 125

Jennings George, 66

JENNINGS Jr.: Augustine, 124

Jenny, 1, 2, 4, 9, 10, 11, 12, 13, 17, 18, 19, 20, 23, 27, 31, 32, 33, 34, 35, 36, 39, 42, 43, 49, 54, 57, 59, 61, 62, 63, 65, 66, 67, 68, 71, 73, 74, 77, 78, 80, 81, 87, 91, 92, 93, 94, 97, 99, 103, 105, 109, 112, 114, 116, 117, 120, 121, 122, 123, 124, 125, 137, 139, 140, 144, 145, 147, 149, 150, 153, 167, 170, 171, 172, 178, 179, 180, 184, 186, 200

Jenny Stones, 61

Jerard, 57, 65, 68, 72, 80, 92, 94, 97, 114, 169, 178, 183

Jeremiah, 32, 41, 50, 55, 67, 74, 81, 92, 97, 100, 101, 102, 115, 119, 133, 155, 181, 195

Jeremy, 34, 115, 116

Jerret, 166

Jerry, 4, 10, 11, 27, 32, 36, 37, 42, 53, 57, 72, 73, 76, 84, 88, 93, 98, 101, 103, 105, 106, 124, 128, 129, 137, 140, 147, 158, 163, 167, 169, 170, 203, 204, 207

Jersey, 61

Jess, 12, 41, 42, 50, 52, 53, 58, 65, 66, 84, 88, 99, 111, 112, 133, 142, 159, 168, 170, 180, 205

Jess (Brent), 192

Jesse, 4, 9, 11, 17, 18, 27, 30, 31, 42, 45, 47, 52, 55, 57, 58, 59, 60, 61, 62, 63, 64, 65, 66, 72, 79, 80, 81, 82, 88, 102, 106, 109, 111, 113, 120, 125, 129, 130, 132, 133, 139, 143, 150, 153, 155, 165, 166, 169, 170, 173, 174, 178, 179, 191, 193, 194, 195, 196, 201

Jessey, 1

JETT: Burkett, 68, 79; Francis, 64; Mariah, 79; Sally, 79; Washington, 79

Jew, 91

Jilly, 126

Jim, 7, 27, 30, 88, 91, 103, 104, 109, 122, 126, 133, 137, 140, 146, 151, 153, 158, 163, 166, 174, 175, 178, 179, 189, 194, 206, 208

Jimmy, 7

Jina__, 191

Jincey, 103, 155

Jinna, 29, 164

Jinny, 57, 69, 72, 116, 126, 130, 149, 155, 157, 164, 174, 178, 183, 188, 192

Jno, 98, 153, 178

Jo, 84, 113, 178
Joan, 5, 6, 20, 24, 73, 140, 143
Joann, 72
Joanna, 180, 188, 195
Joannah, 58
Job, 40
Joe, 1, 2, 3, 4, 16, 17, 18, 29,
    32, 33, 34, 38, 40, 42, 47, 50,
    51, 53, 55, 58, 59, 61, 65, 66,
    70, 72, 80, 82, 93, 94, 97, 98,
    99, 102, 105, 106, 107, 108,
    112, 113, 114, 116, 124, 131,
    133, 138, 143, 145, 147, 149,
    153, 154, 158, 160, 167, 169,
    180, 182, 188, 194, 198, 199,
    200, 205, 208
Joe Jr., 109
Joe Sr., 109
Johanna, 10
John, 29, 32, 36, 38, 40, 41, 42,
    43, 45, 47, 48, 52, 55, 57, 60,
    63, 64, 65, 66, 68, 73, 74, 75,
    76, 77, 79, 80, 84, 87, 88, 90,
    91, 92, 94, 95, 99, 100, 101,
    102, 104, 107, 109, 110, 111,
    112, 113, 116, 117, 118, 119,
    120, 122, 124, 125, 126, 129,
    130, 132, 137, 139, 141, 142,
    143, 144, 145, 146, 147, 149,
    151, 153, 154, 155, 158, 159,
    160, 161, 162, 164, 166, 169,
    170, 172, 173, 174, 175, 177,
    179, 181, 182, 184, 185, 187,
    188, 190, 192, 194, 195, 197,
    199, 200, 201, 202, 203, 205,
    206
JOHN: Benjamin, 183; Daniel,
    138, 139; Thomas, 139
John Dunmore, 28
John Henders, 15
John King, 139
John L. Mathas, 197
John Morphew, 6
John Patrion, 18
Johnny, 123

Johnson, 38
JOHNSON: Bailey, 111, 112,
    114; Bayley N, 204; Charles,
    112; Charles M, 204;
    George, 112, 114, 204;
    George L, 204; Isaac, 55, 58;
    John, 51, 112; Letty, 77;
    Lewis, 94; Lucy, 62; Lydia,
    55; Margaret, 16; Moses, 74,
    77; Presley, 112; Smith, 55;
    Susan H, 148; Turner, 112;
    W. Smith, 42
JOHNSTON: Aaron, 2;
    Frances, 166; Geminia, 52;
    George Alfred, 166; Isaac,
    70, 84; Lucinda, 80; Moses,
    82; Nancy, 80, 166; Sarah,
    166; Smith, 80; Thomas Y,
    166; William, 80, 177;
    Yellis, 166
Jonah, 23
Jonas, 77, 93
Jonathan, 17, 109, 114
Jond, 137
JONES: Betty, 11; Charles,
    124, 155; Dolly, 124; John,
    27; Mary, 128; Nancy, 124;
    Susanna, 128; William, 65,
    124, 128, 155, 177; William
    E., 124
JORDAN: Nancy, 45; Thomas,
    141
Jorina, 120
Joseph, 5, 16, 17, 20, 29, 32,
    33, 44, 62, 64, 66, 71, 74, 75,
    79, 80, 81, 82, 102, 110, 115,
    125, 126, 127, 128, 130, 131,
    139, 149, 154, 158, 159, 160,
    163, 174, 178, 179, 182, 184,
    189, 193, 200, 203, 206
Joseph Jr., 80
Joshiah, 160
Joshua, 7, 15, 17, 36, 37, 39,
    41, 47, 54, 58, 60, 68, 71, 72,
    75, 76, 78, 81, 82, 85, 87, 88,

93, 97, 100, 103, 108, 112, 114, 124, 128, 129, 131, 137, 139, 140, 142, 153, 154, 155, 156, 160, 166, 167, 171, 173, 174, 185, 195, 197, 207
Josiah, 68, 79
Juba, 5, 194
Jubiter, 72
Juby, 4, 24
Juda, 88, 100, 123, 189
Judah, 5, 14, 15, 16, 17, 18, 24, 32, 38, 54, 55, 62, 63, 64, 67, 68, 70, 72, 73, 74, 75, 79, 81, 84, 94, 97, 139, 146, 150, 184
Judah Jr., 139
Jude, 3, 7, 8, 9, 10, 12, 13, 20, 23, 29, 30, 39, 46, 48, 52, 57, 59, 60, 67, 68, 73, 75, 81, 82, 88, 92, 94, 98, 101, 104, 111, 112, 113, 117, 119, 120, 130, 132, 142, 148, 159, 160, 164, 167, 171, 174, 182, 205, 207
Judea, 146, 149
Judia, 59, 89, 104
Judith, 2, 55, 57, 58, 108, 117, 119, 122, 128, 129, 159, 160, 163, 188, 200, 202, 206
Judy, 1, 2, 3, 8, 11, 15, 16, 17, 18, 19, 27, 31, 32, 35, 37, 47, 53, 58, 62, 64, 65, 70, 71, 72, 73, 74, 75, 84, 90, 91, 99, 103, 106, 109, 110, 111, 112, 113, 114, 119, 122, 123, 125, 128, 130, 137, 138, 140, 143, 147, 150, 153, 156, 157, 164, 166, 167, 169, 170, 171, 172, 180, 184, 187, 191, 192, 194, 196, 203, 207
Julia, 155, 158, 173, 174, 206
Julia Ann, 160, 204
Julian, 154
Juliann, 160, 184
Juliet, 124, 127, 130, 165, 198, 202

Jun, 166
June, 120, 129
Junior, 75
Juno, 49, 86, 125
JUNTZFORD: Bronella, 85; Seth, 85
Jupiter, 13, 58, 61

Karney: Bartholomew, 12
Kate, 1, 36, 45, 47, 49, 53, 56, 116
Katherine, 52
Kato, 195
Katy, 123, 178
Kaziah, 36
KEARTON: Anthony, 74, 77
KEEBLE: Hannah, 112; Richard, 112, 115
KEITH: Amanda D., 102; Anderson, 102; Betty, 34; Caty Gallahue, 34; Charlotte Ashmore, 34; George, 102; Isham, 34, 109; James, 109; Joham, 34; John, 101, 102; Joseph D., 102; Judah, 34; Mary I., 109; Mary Isham, 34; Mrs., 109; Peter G., 109; Peyton R., 102; Susan G., 109; Tarlton F., 109; Thomas, 51, 89, 102, 109
Keity, 57
KELLER: Henry, 141
KELLY: Capt John, 208; Capt. John, 154, 198; George P., 154; James W, 154; Jno., 154; John P., 154; Peter C, 197; Richard P., 154
KEMP: Dorothy, 127, 129, 181; Molly, 199
KEMPER: Ann, 56; Anne, 1; Diner, 103; Elizabeth, 203; Jacob, 87, 91; James, 106; John, 56, 57, 100; John Peter, 35; Mary, 196; Susannah, 76; Tilman, 56

KENNARD: Elizabeth, 168, 173, 184, 190, 198, 201; Joshua, 134, 161, 174
KENNER: Elizabeth, 204; George Turbervile, 17; Howson, 17; Judith, 41; Lawrence, 41; Lucy, 41; Rodham, 41, 42
Kepsy, 128
KERFOOT: Daniel S, 208
KERR: Asenath, 202; Betty, 50; Dorcas, 202; John, 51; Peggy Smith, 202; Sara, 56; Sarah, 202
KERR Jr.: John, 50
KERR Sr.: John, 50
Kesiah, 179
Kesse, 27
Kessey, 33
Kessiah, 80
Kezia, 56
Keziah, 15, 31, 32, 112, 113, 178, 188
Kiah, 110
KIBBLE: Fanny Watson, 134
KIDWILL: Mary, 47; William, 47
Killis, 6, 76, 119
KINCAID: Margaret, 159; William, 142, 184, 201; Wm, 184
KINCHELOE: Sarah, 146
KINCHELS: James, 186
King, 11, 44, 56, 57, 122, 169
KING: Jesse, 76; Scitha, 76
Kingston, 74, 126, 134
Kipsey, 109, 117
KIRK: Elizabeth, 20, 30; William, 20, 30
Kit, 47, 194
Kitt, 29, 66, 70, 112, 128
Kitty, 49, 58, 68, 71, 73, 74, 78, 79, 82, 87, 91, 102, 107, 108, 114, 117, 120, 122, 123, 129, 132, 137, 138, 140, 141, 145,

147, 153, 154, 158, 160, 162, 165, 166, 172, 173, 175, 179, 180, 181, 188, 192, 194, 195, 200, 201, 203
Kizzy, 51, 148
KNOX: Elizabeth, 30; Jannett, 30; John, 30, 75, 98; R., 75; Robert, 30, 31, 98; Robert Dade, 30
Kouhey, 93

L. George, 66
L__aed, 138
Lacey, 179, 199
LAKE: Elizabeth, 68
LAMPKIN: Griffin, 169; Jno., 169; Joseph, 169; Peter, 169
Lanam, 193
Lancaster, 15
Lance, 116
Landaman, 36, 38
Landen, 174
Lander, 154
Landern, 127
Landon, 32, 120, 122, 143, 198
LANE: Betsy, 99
LANGSTAN: Reuben, 145
Lanom, 193
Larkin, 68
LATHAM: Frances, 202; Franklin, 172; Jesse, 184; Thomas, 112
LATHRAM: Betsy, 167; Betty, 167; Franklin, 167; John, 167
Lattice, 146
Laura, 158, 162, 170
LAURANCE: Edward, 31, 32; John, 31; Peter, 31; Richard, 32
LAURANCE Sr.: Edward, 31
LAURENCE: Mason, 184
Laurinda, 102, 160, 179
Laury, 77

Lavina, 117, 131, 137, 138, 147, 155, 166, 173, 184
Lavinia, 174, 179
Lawrence, 195, 206
LAWRENCE: Elizabeth, 207; Rhodam Tulloss, 32
Lawrey, 76
Lawry, 72
Lawsey, 150
Lawson, 105, 118
LAWSON: Anna Steptoe, 12; Catherine, 133; Epaphroditus, 12; James, 194, 204; John, 54
Lazarus, 143
Leage, 35
Lealy, 131
Leander, 156, 189
Leanna, 39, 122
Leannar, 43
LEARY: William, 104
Leda, 2
Lede, 199
Ledea, 52
Lee, 101, 105
LEE: Ann G, 197, 206; Ann G., 173; Charles, 180; E E, 206; Elizabeth E., 173; Fanny, 173, 197; Hancock, 72, 155, 173, 206; Henry, 81, 85; Jno A, 206; John A., 173; John H., 173; Mary, 163, 173; Mary W, 173, 181, 197; Pamela, 173, 206; Thomas L., 173; Willis, 131
Leeva, 179
Lege, 35, 116
Leipie, 21
Lelah, 9, 41, 85
Lelia, 43
LEMERT: Lewis, 134, 140
Lemmon, 12, 59, 180
LEMMON: George, 194
Lemon, 122, 126, 185
Len, 83, 101, 129

Lena, 73
Lenai, 178
Lennen, 122
Lenny, 80
Leoderick, 160
Leoman, 60
Leonard, 89, 112, 125
LEONARD: Matthew, 77, 79, 81
Leonora, 11
Leotes, 17
Lereno, 37
Leroy, 123, 125
Let, 5, 46, 59, 81, 92, 149
Lett, 6, 7, 9, 16, 17, 23, 24, 28, 31, 41, 42, 46, 50, 53, 58, 59, 62, 64, 65, 66, 79, 89, 101, 116, 124, 133, 151, 171, 184, 205
Letta, 116
Lettice, 7, 15, 20, 42, 44, 52, 55, 65, 68, 76, 158, 186, 187, 204
Letty, 8, 17, 18, 36, 37, 38, 42, 49, 61, 70, 72, 86, 87, 89, 99, 108, 113, 121, 124, 140, 142, 145, 155, 158, 163, 165, 166, 173, 174, 181, 186, 193, 195, 200
Levi, 129, 153, 162, 174, 193
Levin, 119
Levina, 17, 36, 40, 43, 56, 70, 82, 119, 123, 124, 129, 140, 173, 174, 194, 195, 203
Levinah, 145
Levinia, 162
Levy, 103, 119
Lew, 84, 111, 145
Lewie, 3, 51
Lewis, 9, 16, 18, 20, 22, 23, 33, 41, 42, 43, 46, 50, 54, 56, 58, 59, 60, 62, 63, 65, 66, 69, 72, 73, 74, 75, 76, 79, 80, 81, 82, 85, 86, 91, 93, 94, 95, 97, 99, 100, 101, 102, 103, 104, 105,

106, 107, 108, 109, 110, 112, 116, 118, 119, 122, 123, 124, 125, 126, 127, 131, 133, 134, 137, 138, 139, 140, 142, 144, 145, 146, 147, 149, 152, 153, 155, 156, 158, 161, 162, 163, 164, 165, 166, 167, 172, 174, 178, 179, 180, 181, 183, 184, 188, 189, 191, 192, 193, 194, 196, 197, 201, 202, 203, 206, 207, 208

LEWIS: Betsy, 146; Fanny, 125; James, 67

Lewis Blue, 189

Lewis Willis, 83, 90

Li_as, 93

Lias, 191

Lid, 8, 68, 80

Lidda, 15, 97, 108, 112, 141

Liddy, 20, 39, 44, 83, 88, 94, 153, 199

Lidia, 41, 42, 105, 111, 137, 160, 167

Lige, 57, 134

Lila, 116

Lilay, 116

Lilly, 44, 52, 171

Limego, 97

Limus, 79

Lina, 11, 93, 154, 177

Linah, 179

Linda, 58, 65, 72, 128, 206

Lindy, 60

Linia, 178, 180

Linn, 91

Linna, 38, 93, 116, 183, 184, 198

Linney, 39, 92, 101

Linny, 16, 89, 166

Lipion, 115

Lish, 102, 107

Liss, 25

Littleton, 69, 162, 165

Liverpool, 80

Livina, 54

Liz, 45, 68, 118

Liza, 47, 110, 116, 117, 118, 128, 161, 163, 168, 179

Lizzy, 42, 45, 51, 101, 127

LOMAX: George, 109

London, 20, 23, 33, 35, 73, 132, 148, 202, 208

LORD: Mary S., 140

Lorina, 120

Lorinda, 156

Lorindro, 153

Lorry, 58, 141

Lott, 11, 39, 70, 131, 164

Lotty, 70

Lou, 88, 92

Louisa, 89, 117, 122, 125, 137, 140, 143, 148, 153, 154, 156, 162, 179, 188, 189, 195, 204, 206

Louiza, 191, 204

LOVE: Mary, 86

Lovice, 164

LOWRY: George, 117; Nancy, 117

Luanna, 165

LUCAS: Elizabeth, 204; Sarah, 103

Luce, 6, 7, 11, 16, 20, 21, 22, 23, 29, 30, 54, 61, 65, 72, 73, 81, 106, 117, 122, 149

Luce Jr., 16

Lucia, 18

Lucinda, 9, 21, 66, 67, 75, 79, 81, 88, 90, 93, 97, 98, 107, 108, 110, 111, 122, 123, 126, 128, 129, 131, 133, 145, 146, 149, 151, 153, 160, 162, 170, 173, 174, 193, 200, 202, 206

Lucindy, 64

LUCKETT: John D., 60, 61; Mary, 61; Nancy, 61, 187, 203; Thomas, 61, 150; Thomas H., 60, 61; William, 60, 61, 159

Lucretia, 112, 125, 140, 197

Lucy, 1, 2, 3, 4, 5, 6, 7, 9, 10, 11, 12, 13, 15, 16, 17, 18, 19, 20, 21, 22, 23, 24, 28, 32, 33, 34, 37, 38, 39, 42, 43, 45, 47, 49, 50, 51, 53, 54, 55, 56, 57, 58, 59, 60, 61, 62, 63, 65, 66, 67, 68, 69, 70, 72, 73, 74, 75, 77, 78, 79, 80, 82, 83, 85, 86, 87, 88, 90, 91, 92, 93, 94, 97, 99, 100, 101, 102, 104, 105, 106, 108, 109, 111, 112, 113, 114, 115, 116, 117, 118, 119, 120, 122, 123, 124, 125, 127, 128, 129, 130, 131, 132, 137, 138, 140, 143, 144, 145, 146, 148, 149, 150, 153, 154, 155, 156, 157, 159, 160, 161, 162, 163, 165, 166, 167, 169, 170, 171, 173, 174, 175, 177, 178, 180, 181, 182, 183, 184, 185, 188, 190, 192, 194, 196, 197, 199, 200, 204, 205, 206
Lucy Ann, 192
Lucy Cook, 127, 181
Lucy M, 188
Lucy Margaret, 181
LUDDITH: Levi, 116; Peggy, 116
Ludwell, 174, 193
Luiasa, 87
Luinsa, 11
Luisa, 200
Luke, 21, 69, 77, 118, 119, 194
Lunnum, 156
LUNSFORD: Amos, 28
Lurilly, 68
Lute, 81
LUTTRELL: Winnefred, 32
Lyd, 14, 110
Lyda, 82, 153
Lydda, 39, 120
Lydia, 2, 12, 15, 18, 40, 41, 43, 45, 46, 52, 65, 66, 67, 71, 73, 74, 79, 80, 81, 89, 91, 101, 110, 116, 117, 121, 122, 125,

126, 128, 129, 131, 134, 139, 140, 142, 146, 148, 153, 166, 168, 174, 182, 188, 202, 204
Lymas, 29
Lymos, 37
Lynas, 137
Lynn, 44, 59; Jeffrey, 129
LYNN: John, 45
Lynna, 65
Lyttia, 153
Lyttie, 153

MacKAY: Moses, 141
MACORMACK: John, 32; Stephen, 32
MADDUX: Craven, 128; Elizabeth, 8, 70; Richard, 70; Thomas, 70, 164; Thomas B., 70; Thomas L., 128; William, 103, 104
Madison, 160
Magdalena, 188
MAGRUDER: Ninian, 178
Mahala, 116, 124, 125, 127, 129, 146, 149, 150, 152, 158, 160, 162, 163, 187, 199, 205, 206, 208
Mahalah, 120
Mahalia, 183
Mahaly, 138, 147, 186, 192
Mahanda, 169
Mahilda, 205
Maicah, 85, 154
Maitilda, 126
Major, 133, 192
Malinda, 51, 52, 59, 75, 89, 94, 106, 109, 122, 141, 146, 148, 149, 151, 152, 153, 159, 177, 178, 179, 190, 194
Malindy, 120, 150
Mall, 35
MALLORY: Betsey, 76; Clement C., 60; James, 76; Jane, 37, 41; Lucy, 37, 41; Philip, 41

Mammy, 67, 98
Manaford, 207
Manah, 109
Manamy, 81
MANATREE: Jacob, 69
Manawill, 23
Manuel, 12, 22, 52, 54, 72, 73,
    74, 88, 102, 107, 119, 128,
    131, 133, 139, 148, 154, 160,
    162, 164, 169, 170, 177, 180,
    188
March, 28
Marcia, 155, 173, 174
Marcus, 178, 179, 188
Marcy, 92, 95
Margaret, 112, 118, 182, 188,
    194, 204
Marge, 105, 172
Margery, 143, 158, 161
Maria, 59, 61, 71, 72, 73, 76,
    77, 85, 87, 93, 98, 100, 101,
    102, 103, 111, 112, 114, 118,
    119, 122, 123, 124, 125, 126,
    128, 129, 131, 134, 140, 141,
    143, 144, 148, 149, 153, 155,
    160, 162, 166, 170, 174, 177,
    178, 181, 182, 184, 185, 187,
    188, 190, 192, 194, 195, 198,
    200, 207
Mariah, 21, 41, 58, 60, 61, 65,
    67, 70, 75, 81, 82, 84, 92, 97,
    98, 104, 113, 120, 122, 123,
    124, 127, 128, 129, 130, 143,
    144, 145, 146, 149, 163, 165,
    169, 171, 172, 181, 188, 190,
    192, 193, 194, 203, 206
Mariam, 139
Marian, 94
Marjory, 196
Mark, 66, 67, 81, 90, 118, 156,
    179, 204
MARKHAM: Catey, 17; John,
    29
Marlin, 133
Marlina, 66

Marmaduke, 21
MAROGEE: Thomas, 196
MARR: Daniel, 193, 195;
    Susanna, 193
Marsh Run Jack, 130
Marshall, 101, 102, 120, 158
MARSHALL: Charles, 37, 77;
    Lucy, 77, 187
Martain, 95
Martha, 17, 36, 37, 38, 59, 60,
    73, 158, 165, 178, 179, 185,
    202, 204
Martha Jane, 185
Martin, 55, 57, 61, 86, 88, 93,
    97, 109, 112, 118, 131, 139,
    149, 152, 153, 154, 185, 188,
    206, 207, 208
MARTIN: Alfred, 179;
    Andrew, 161; Ann G., 142;
    Catherine, 179; Charles, 163;
    Eliza Ann, 155, 179;
    Elizabeth, 165; Elizabeth Mt
    joy, 32; Emily, 179; Francis,
    178; George, 163, 202, 207;
    Henry, 165; James Galliton,
    155; Jane, 179; John, 165,
    166, 207; Louisa, 165;
    Melvin, 179; Robert L, 204;
    Robert L., 179; Samuel, 178;
    William, 163
Mary, 13, 17, 20, 22, 23, 28, 31,
    32, 33, 35, 36, 37, 41, 43, 44,
    46, 49, 50, 51, 54, 56, 57, 59,
    60, 64, 65, 66, 68, 69, 70, 75,
    79, 80, 81, 82, 83, 85, 86, 87,
    88, 89, 90, 92, 93, 94, 95, 97,
    98, 99, 100, 101, 102, 104,
    105, 109, 111, 113, 117, 118,
    119, 120, 122, 123, 124, 127,
    128, 129, 132, 133, 134, 137,
    138, 139, 140, 142, 143, 145,
    147, 150, 152, 153, 155, 156,
    157, 158, 159, 160, 162, 164,
    165, 166, 167, 169, 170, 172,
    173, 174, 178, 179, 180, 181,

34

182, 185, 186, 188, 192, 193, 194, 195, 200, 201, 202, 203, 206, 207
Mary Ann, 70, 159, 164, 169, 192
Mary Anne, 111, 188
Mary Cook, 127, 181
Mary Finley, 180
Mary Jane, 164, 192
Mary Jones, 13
Mary___, 86
Maryann, 181
Masiah, 149
Masner, 200
Mason, 20, 31, 73, 99, 101, 127, 145, 147, 160, 179, 181, 191
MASON: Peter, 55; William, 66
MASSIE: Asa, 65, 69, 125; Benjamin M., 69; Benjamin Morehead, 65; Dolly, 65, 125; John, 65, 69; Joseph, 69; Josias, 65; Molly, 69; Nimrod, 65, 168; Polly, 69; Robert, 65; Robert F., 141, 168; Samuel, 65, 69; Thomas, 65, 66, 69, 92
Mat, 165
Mathas: James, 197; John L, 197; Nancy, 197; William Jackson, 197
Mathers, 144
Matilda, 39, 52, 61, 97, 101, 106, 108, 110, 114, 118, 119, 122, 124, 127, 134, 140, 144, 145, 147, 148, 149, 153, 160, 162, 164, 165, 166, 170, 173, 174, 178, 179, 188, 192, 197
Matit___, 126
Matt, 10, 11, 154, 165
Matthew, 32, 42, 65, 92, 101, 153
MATTHEWS: Sally, 40

MATTHIS: Alice, 5; Dudly, 5; Elizabeth, 5; Robert, 4, 5; Sarah, 5
Maude, 20
MAUZY: Betty, 14; Elizabeth, 76, 203; George, 76; Henry, 76, 79; Jemimah, 53; John, 3, 4, 5, 6, 14, 56, 76; Mary, 5, 6, 30; Molly, 3, 14; Myma, 42; Peggy, 3, 14; Peter, 76; Sally, 7, 14, 19, 29; Thomas, 102; William, 76
MAUZY Sr.: Henry, 76
Mawser, 174
Mazer, 4
McCLANAHAM: James, 57, 66
McCONCHIE: Alexander, 107, 109, 156; Ann, 107; Mary Ann, 156; Robert, 102, 156
McCONNEL: Alex, 165
McCORMICK: Elizabeth, 178; John, 138, 139, 178, 188; John W., 154; Peter B., 178; Stephen, 33, 105; William, 139
McDANIEL: Hannah, 197
McDONALD: Lott, 208
McFARLAND: John, 71
McHarada, 111
McKAY: Betty, 27
McKINNY: John, 46; Susanna, 46
McKINNY Sr.: John, 48
McLEAREN: Archibald, 150
McLEOD: William, 178
McMULLEN: Archibald, 123
McNEALE: William W., 177
McNISH: David, 70, 92; Horatio, 92, 94, 104, 113, 130, 142; Horatio W., 98; Polley W., 98; Polly, 92, 94; William, 94, 104, 113, 130;

35

William Maudaroisky, 92;
William W., 98
Mealey, 79
Mehala, 123
Melacinda, 133
Melia, 68, 118
Melinda, 103, 123, 160, 166,
167, 173, 174, 194, 202, 203,
204
Mercer, 32, 45
Meshach, 80, 85, 100, 107
METCALF: Charles, 57; Mrs.,
105
Miccah, 30
Michael, 67, 68, 78, 101, 161
Mildred, 125, 138, 162, 188,
194
Miles, 141, 158
Miley, 82
Mill, 3, 10, 14, 15, 19, 46, 56,
65, 107, 110, 111
Milla, 44, 153
Miller, 100, 172
MILLER: Elizabeth, 1; John,
103; Simon, 6, 7; Thomas,
187
Milly, 1, 2, 9, 10, 11, 12, 13,
15, 16, 17, 18, 19, 22, 31, 34,
36, 37, 38, 39, 41, 42, 44, 46,
47, 51, 52, 53, 54, 55, 57, 58,
59, 60, 62, 64, 65, 66, 68, 69,
71, 73, 75, 76, 78, 80, 81, 86,
87, 90, 93, 95, 97, 98, 99,
101, 102, 103, 104, 105, 106,
108, 109, 110, 111, 112, 113,
114, 119, 122, 124, 125, 126,
127, 129, 131, 133, 134, 137,
140, 141, 142, 143, 144, 145,
147, 154, 155, 156, 157, 159,
164, 165, 167, 168, 170, 171,
173, 174, 175, 179, 182, 183,
188, 189, 191, 195, 197, 200,
202, 204, 207, 208
Milly Jr., 160
Milly Sr., 160

Milton, 147, 158, 160, 186
Mima, 19, 42, 43, 50, 53, 54,
71, 73, 85, 89, 92, 109, 112,
122, 125, 133, 137, 148, 150,
153, 163, 169, 173, 192, 194,
206
Mimah, 29, 143
Mime, 31, 32, 146
Mimia, 153
Mimum, 119
Mimy, 15, 31, 49, 64, 131, 158,
160, 162, 174, 179, 199
MINATREE: Jacob, 81
Miner, 94, 98, 104
Mingo, 4, 36, 37, 193, 195
Minnah, 145
Minny, 18, 50
Minor, 70, 92, 106, 113, 130
Minta, 44, 68, 101, 112
MINTER: Jacob, 38; John, 16,
38; Joseph, 11, 12, 51;
Joseph T, 189; Mary, 11;
Matilda, 188; William, 38
Minty, 46, 83, 143, 153
Mira, 109, 113
Mirah, 182
Miriah, 118
Miriam, 60, 137
Mises, 128
MITCHELL: Elizabeth, 199
MOFFETT: John H, 118; Sarah
Smith, 118
Moileller, 90
Moll, 2, 8, 11, 12, 13, 21, 22,
23, 29, 31, 32, 37, 44, 50, 67,
68
Molly, 6, 17, 30, 31, 33, 49, 61,
62, 64, 65, 70, 75, 77, 100,
103, 105, 111, 112, 116, 123,
137, 140, 147, 149, 153, 166,
168, 174, 175, 193, 195
Moncury, 126
Monday, 27, 28
MONDAY: Charles, 71; Mary,
71

Monica, 129
Monick, 71
Monnick, 58
MONROE: Daniel, 36
Mood, 145
Moona, 205
Moore, 188
MOORE: Hanna, 207; Ruth, 207; Sally, 76; Samuel, 76
MOOREHEAD: Presley W, 186
Mooter, 131
Mordeca, 131
Mordecai, 128
MOREHEAD: Alexander, 5, 131, 140; Ann, 32; Armistead, 27, 155; Capt. Charles, 28; Charles, 27, 51, 131, 155; Elizabeth, 27; George, 155; James, 27; Joel, 131; John, 5, 131, 155; Lewis, 186; Lydia, 51; Mary, 27, 51; Peggy, 51; Presley, 27, 151; Presley W, 186; Samuel, 51, 52; Samuel R., 51; Susan, 186; Turner, 27; William, 131, 155; Wilmauth, 51
Morgan, 81, 82
MORGAN: James, 170; Joseph, 30, 41, 64; Sarah, 163; Simeon, 41; Simon, 44, 108; Susan, 140
Moriah, 24
MORIN: John, 71; Sally, 71
Morris, 107, 111
MORRIS, 76, 80; Alexander, 114; Hannah R., 114; Polly, 113; Richard L, 193; Richard P., 114; Sander, 109, 113; William, 113, 145
MORRISON: Hyram, 171; Polly, 171; Sarah, 171
Morten, 173, 174

Morton, 24, 30, 140, 142, 153, 173, 184, 200, 201; William, 194
Mosby, 27
Mose, 32
Moses, 7, 8, 9, 10, 11, 12, 13, 16, 17, 18, 20, 24, 28, 29, 30, 32, 34, 35, 39, 41, 42, 44, 45, 47, 54, 57, 58, 59, 62, 63, 64, 66, 67, 69, 70, 72, 73, 75, 76, 77, 79, 80, 81, 85, 88, 92, 95, 100, 103, 104, 105, 106, 107, 110, 112, 118, 121, 122, 123, 124, 126, 129, 130, 131, 133, 137, 139, 140, 141, 143, 147, 150, 153, 155, 157, 158, 159, 160, 161, 162, 165, 169, 184, 186, 188, 194, 195
Mountain Rate, 123
Mournfull, 103
Mourning, 55
MOXLEY: Hannah, 76, 80, 158; Jermiah, 76, 80; John, 76; Selby, 80, Sibbella, 76
Mu__eah, 8
MURPHEY: John, 6
MURRAY: Jno, 153; John, 149; Ralph, 91, 92; Reuben, 142; Samuel, 189
MURREY: James, 27
MURRY: James, 24; Ralph, 24
MYERS: Sarah, 142
Myme, 133
Mymey, 85, 100
Mymy, 38
MYRES: Peggy, 59

N__BLE: Peggy, 11
Nace, 29, 50, 69, 74, 79, 117, 128, 143, 145, 147, 160, 162, 172, 188, 195, 201, 206
Nacy, 188
Nair, 179
Nan, 1, 2, 3, 6, 8, 11, 12, 13, 17, 19, 20, 21, 22, 28, 30, 31, 32,

36, 37, 39, 40, 42, 43, 46, 47,
56, 59, 63, 64, 76, 104, 116,
123, 178, 194
Nan Nelly, 161
Nance, 39, 41, 52, 70, 72, 98,
103, 119, 138, 147, 159, 184,
189
Nancy, 2, 3, 16, 27, 42, 53, 57,
58, 62, 64, 65, 66, 67, 68, 69,
70, 71, 72, 73, 74, 76, 79, 80,
81, 86, 87, 88, 91, 92, 94, 95,
101, 103, 104, 105, 106, 109,
110, 114, 115, 116, 120, 121,
122, 123, 125, 126, 129, 132,
134, 137, 138, 140, 141, 142,
143, 144, 145, 147, 148, 150,
153, 155, 157, 158, 159, 160,
164, 165, 166, 172, 173, 174,
178, 179, 181, 182, 185, 186,
187, 188, 189, 192, 194, 195,
197, 201, 205, 206
Nancy Buckner, 67
Nancy Jr, 80
Nancy Mathas, 197
Nancy Sr., 80
Nann, 45
Nanny, 2, 4, 28, 38, 39, 43, 44,
53, 55, 76, 84, 103, 108, 112,
121, 125, 129, 132, 144, 151,
153, 154, 166, 178
Narassa, 66
Narthey, 103
NASH: Abner, 133; Elijah, 15;
Epaphreditus, 133; John,
133; Travers, 133; Traverse,
133; Traverse C., 133;
Travis, 154
Nassau, 140
Nat, 50, 52, 59, 120, 132, 134,
173, 174, 183, 197
Nat Grace, 97
Nat Jr., 132
Nathan, 58, 172, 173, 195
Nathaniel, 117, 155, 195
Natus, 99, 113

NEALE: Hannah, 117; James,
61; Joseph, 29; Mary, 29;
Matthew, 74; Peggy, 146;
Richard, 61; Thomas, 126;
William, 61, 100
NEAVIL: George, 11, 12;
Mary, 11
Ned, 1, 2, 6, 9, 13, 17, 23, 31,
34, 36, 37, 38, 41, 42, 50, 51,
53, 54, 58, 59, 60, 61, 63, 64,
68, 71, 75, 76, 77, 78, 83, 89,
93, 94, 97, 99, 101, 102, 105,
107, 109, 110, 111, 113, 115,
116, 119, 122, 123, 131, 137,
139, 143, 148, 166, 169, 170,
171, 172, 173, 179, 180, 188,
194, 196, 197, 206
Ned Jr., 66
Ned S__te, 10, 12
Ned Sr., 66
Nell, 4, 5, 16, 29, 30, 32, 33,
34, 35, 36, 42, 43, 46, 55, 56,
57, 66, 68, 70, 73, 89, 99,
100, 113, 126, 163
Nelly, 29, 41, 53, 66, 68, 70,
72, 74, 79, 92, 93, 94, 100,
104, 106, 109, 113, 115, 123,
124, 127, 128, 129, 130, 154,
161, 162, 165, 166, 167, 173,
174, 178, 179, 197, 203, 205,
207, 208
Nelson, 50, 51, 56, 59, 64, 69,
72, 115, 141, 163, 165, 183,
188, 190, 197
NELSON: Caty, 10; James,
102, 115; Jeminia, 29; John,
30; Jos, 13; Lettice, 29;
Margaret, 29; Sarah, 29;
William, 14
NELSON Jr.: John, 29
NELSON Sr.: John, 41
Neptune, 51, 52
NEUGENT: Edward, 36, 38,
39, 40, 47; Thomas, 36, 37,
39

38

NEWBY: Betty, 40
NEWHOUSE: Polly, 54
Newman, 66
NEWMAN: Esther, 76
Newton, 52, 54, 156, 157, 186, 199
Nicholas, 38, 62, 80, 113
Nicholas Ball, 13
Nicholas George, 99
Nick, 32, 33, 53, 80, 111, 167, 174
NICKLESS: Thomas, 65
NICOLS: John, 8
Nim, 86
Nimrod, 31, 49, 121, 170, 192
Ninnel, 188
Niten, 76
Noble, 179, 203
NOLIN: William, 139
Nora, 50, 158
Norah, 32, 70
Norfolk Tom, 10, 11
NORMAN: Edward, 55
NORRIS: Catherine, 70; Elizabeth, 70; Ellin, 70; Hannah, 70; Mary, 70; Sarah, 70; Septimus, 59, 154; Thaddeus, 153, 172, 177, 179, 201; William, 67, 70
NUGENT: Ann, 30
Nully, 4
NUTT: Richard, 106
Nutty, 183

O'BANNON: John W, 184; Joseph, 195, 206; Presley, 184; Thomas, 184; William, 184
OBANNON: Amistead, 150; Andrew, 13; Col. John, 37; George, 13; Isham, 126; J.L., 13; Jno, 13; John, 13, 52, 53, 107, 108; Joseph, 172, 173; Lydda, 52; Lyddia, 52;

Mary, 117; Minor, 117; Pamenas B., 172; Parmerus, 148; Samuel, 13; Sylvia, 56; William, 52, 79, 91, 97, 101, 175
OBANON: Bryan, 2; Fanny, 17; John, 2; Mary, 19; William, 2
OBANON Sr: John, 10
Obid, 193, 195
ODEN: Vincent, 76
ODEY: Nancy, 130
OGLEVIE: Leah Foley, 52; Presley Foley, 52; Susanna Foley, 52
Oliva, 195
Oliver, 10, 11, 88
OLIVER: Elizabeth, 123; Mary, 131
Olly, 108
Orange, 98
Original, 31
Orrick, 61
Osborn, 148
Oscar, 198
Osten, 57
Ovid, 81, 82, 98
OWEN: Aaron, 106; Mason, 193; Nathaniel, 91, 100
OWENS: Aaron, 106; Ephraim, 87; Jeremiah, 12; Nathaniel, 91
Ozborn, 141

Page, 113, 121, 178, 179, 184
PAGE: George, 159
Pallas, 190
PALMER: Sally, 198
Pamela, 160
Paris, 149
Parker, 105
PARKER: Alexander, 31, 61; Amey, 31, 61; Eliza Scott, 61; Elizabeth, 31; Judith, 61; Judith A., 84; Lucy, 31, 61;

Richard, 31, 61; Scott, 31; William, 13, 31, 61
Parkerson, 164
PARRIS: John, 84
Pat, 1, 2, 4, 10, 11, 13, 17, 18, 36, 37, 38, 41, 49, 50, 59, 73, 76, 79, 88, 89, 90, 102, 107, 149
PATE: Elizabeth, 162
Pati_on, 126
Patience, 10, 11, 13, 36, 38, 42, 72, 73, 74, 79, 105, 129, 130, 131, 133, 140, 145, 165, 190
Patince, 154
Patison, 134
Patrick, 120, 194
Patrick Maguire, 10
Patsy, 97, 115, 123, 151, 154, 166, 189, 192, 194
Patt, 101
Patta, 68
Patterson, 66
PATTERSON: John, 138
Patty, 56, 65, 74, 77, 80, 85, 117, 126, 127, 142, 153, 154, 162, 165, 167, 173, 175, 181, 187, 196, 200
Paul, 47, 67, 77, 142, 144, 154, 163, 194
PAYNE: Agnes, 44; Albert, 131; Benjamin, 55; Catherine, 131; Daniel F., 111; Elizabeth Johnston, 80; Francis, 137, 147, 158; Jesse, 158; John, 106, 108, 113; Mrs., 137; Presley, 137; Susanna, 55; Thomas, 153; Turner, 137, 141; William, 19, 137
PEAKE: Elizabeth, 19; John, 19; Mary, 19; Sally, 19; Thomas, 19
PEARCE: John, 107
PEARLE: Martha, 30; Samuel, 179, 200; William, 30, 31

Peg, 9, 10, 11, 12, 13, 17, 18, 20, 29, 30, 31, 32, 33, 34, 42, 43, 45, 46, 50, 51, 53, 54, 57, 58, 59, 61, 64, 68, 70, 86, 88, 89, 90, 92, 94, 98, 104, 111, 116, 118
Pegg, 68
Peggy, 35, 53, 56, 66, 69, 79, 80, 84, 88, 89, 91, 94, 103, 104, 108, 109, 112, 114, 116, 125, 134, 137, 149, 153, 158, 166
Pelia, 185
PENDELTON: George, 110; Sally, 110
Pender, 103, 208
Penelope, 87
Pennillapy, 22
Penny, 17, 32, 42
PENQUITE: William, 166
PEPPER: Jeremiah, 115; Lucy, 42
Perry, 59, 132, 180
Peter, 2, 3, 4, 7, 8, 9, 10, 11, 12, 14, 17, 24, 27, 28, 31, 32, 35, 36, 38, 39, 41, 42, 43, 47, 49, 53, 54, 55, 56, 58, 59, 65, 72, 73, 74, 76, 78, 79, 80, 81, 82, 86, 87, 88, 89, 90, 92, 98, 100, 101, 102, 104, 107, 108, 110, 111, 112, 114, 117, 121, 122, 124, 125, 126, 127, 129, 131, 133, 138, 140, 141, 142, 146, 149, 150, 151, 153, 158, 159, 160, 162, 163, 164, 165, 166, 178, 179, 180, 181, 182, 183, 184, 186, 187, 188, 189, 191, 192, 194, 196, 199, 201, 202, 204, 205
PETER: Samuel, 94
Peter Black, 80
Peter Hawkins, 31
Peter Jr., 126
Peter Sr., 126

PETERS: Ann, 167; Elizabeth, 167, 191; Frances, 138; Henry, 147, 167; James, 21, 76, 147, 150, 167, 179; Jesse, 147, 167; John, 21, 28, 55; Lewis, 21; Margaret, 167; Mary, 50, 147, 167; Nancy, 55, 147; Nathaniel, 21; Nimrod, 21; Peggy, 147, 191; Priscilla, 147, 167, 191; Susannah, 99; William, 21
Peyton, 114
PEYTON: Ann, 141; C., 168; Capt Henry, 148; Chandler, 148, 157, 200; Henry, 122, 148
Pharoah, 77
Phebe, 28, 41, 95, 120, 123, 132, 145, 146, 185, 199
Phil, 1, 2, 3, 4, 11, 21, 35, 43, 45, 50, 53, 56, 60, 61, 68, 86, 87, 94, 95, 106, 109, 114, 133, 144, 149, 156, 166, 167, 174, 194
Philip, 41, 75, 76, 81, 97, 120, 123, 162
Phillip, 52, 53, 67, 82, 83, 128, 153, 159, 203
PHILLIPS: Ann, 118, 195, 197, 204; Barton, 118, 197; Elizabeth, 21; Fanny, 118; Frances, 197; John, 118; John P., 197; Lucy, 118, 197; Richard, 118, 197; William, 105, 115, 118, 197
Phillis, 4, 5, 6, 7, 9, 10, 11, 12, 14, 18, 20, 27, 28, 32, 33, 35, 41, 42, 44, 47, 49, 59, 62, 63, 64, 65, 68, 69, 74, 78, 79, 81, 82, 88, 90, 92, 94, 102, 103, 105, 106, 107, 110, 112, 115, 130, 131, 138, 144, 146, 148, 150, 151, 159, 160, 172, 182, 193, 196, 200
Philly, 116

Phoebe, 109, 114, 189
PICKETT: Anna, 54; Betsy B, 84; Capt. William, 143; Caroline, 119; Elizabeth, 119, 163; George Blackwell, 77; Jno, 28; Lavinia, 119; Lucy, 119; Martin, 77, 80; Sandford, 183; Sanford, 57; Sarah, 4; Steptoe, 77, 107; William, 4, 57, 67, 119, 137; William S, 54; William Sanford, 56
PICKETT Sr.: William, 139
PIERCE: John, 5, 37; Lusanna, 37; Peter, 5, 37; Robert, 57; Rosanna, 37; Rosannah, 5; Susannah, 5
PILCHER: Daniel, 112
Pindar, 27
PINKARD: Charles, 112, 119, 187; Mildred, 28; Sarah, 119
PINKSTONE: Frances, 85; Henry, 77, 85
Pinter, 47
Plato, 30
Pleasant, 17, 55, 58, 72
Poess, 30, 41
Poll, 16, 56, 59, 71, 72, 74, 91, 111
POLLARD: Isaac, 140; Jane, 116; Mildred, 116, 123; PH, 126
Polly, 38, 53, 66, 67, 68, 73, 75, 76, 78, 79, 80, 81, 87, 92, 109, 110, 112, 117, 128, 129, 131, 133, 140, 149, 151, 153, 154, 155, 156, 159, 160, 162, 163, 174, 175, 185, 186, 188, 193, 194, 200, 205
Polly Wanser, 154
Poly dore, 66
Pomp, 86, 162
Pompey, 58, 61, 67, 69, 70, 72, 74, 80, 109, 158, 173, 178, 182, 199

41

Poor House, 159

PORTER: Agga, 162; Aggatha, 75; Betty, 58; Charles, 58, 60; Ebbin, 56; Eli, 60, 88; Eppy, 60; Eve, 2; Hannah, 42, 53; Jane, 42; Jean, 42; Lewis, 140; Martha, 88; Martin, 75, 149; Sally, 130; Samuel, 3, 91, 149; Sarah, 91; Sukey, 91; Thomas, 58, 59, 60, 91, 192; William, 58, 91, 149

Pose, 99

Potter, 107, 111

POWELL: Burr, 78, 114, 115; Catherine, 106, 114, 115; Kitty, 49

Prank, 43

Presley, 178

Press, 76

PRESTON: William, 93

PRICE: Bennett, 13, 20

PRICHARD: Peggy, 17; Stephen, 17

PRIEST: John, 99, 102; Sarah, 32, 47; Thomas, 21, 47, 49; William, 21, 22, 194

Primus, 146, 151

Prince, 13, 20, 41, 42, 53, 185, 186

Priscilla, 32, 50, 59, 139, 148, 153, 160, 188, 194, 200

Priss, 1, 2, 17, 32, 42, 50, 73, 75, 77, 80, 83, 92, 94, 104, 113, 124, 130, 142, 143, 148, 156

Prissy, 57, 163

Pumely, 115

Punch, 49

QUARLES: Betty, 9, 10

QUEENSBERRY: Elizabeth, 126; ES, 126; James, 126

Quinty, 93

Rachel, 10, 11, 12, 17, 18, 23, 28, 29, 31, 33, 36, 37, 39, 40, 42, 43, 49, 51, 52, 53, 54, 55, 56, 58, 59, 62, 66, 68, 70, 71, 72, 74, 80, 81, 82, 84, 86, 87, 88, 89, 93, 97, 103, 104, 105, 106, 108, 111, 116, 120, 124, 126, 127, 129, 132, 133, 137, 139, 140, 145, 147, 151, 163, 166, 169, 170, 172, 174, 178, 179, 181, 184, 188, 190, 191, 192, 195, 198, 199, 205, 206

Rachel Jr, 207

Rafe, 62

RALEY: Elizabeth, 109; Thomas, 109, 115

Ralf, 149

Ralph, 11, 12, 22, 53, 80, 86, 87, 92, 94, 110, 111, 112, 139, 153, 180, 196, 199, 204

Randall, 191, 199

Randell, 116

Randolph, 53, 158

RANDOLPH: Col Robert, 188; Robert, 185, 198

Ransdell, 192

RANSDELL: Capt. Wharton, 34; Chilton, 94, 197, 201; Edward, 32; John, 32; Maj. Thomas, 50; Margarett, 32; Mary, 27; Sarah, 32; Thomas, 32, 44; Wharton, 32; William, 13, 32, 34

RANSDELL Jr.: Wharton, 33

Rass, 112

RATCLIFF: Charles, 145

Rather, 98

Ratter, 81, 98

Raughley, 59

Rawliegh, 155

Raxee, 142

Ray, 52

RAY: Sarah, 21; Thomas, 101

READ: Rebecca, 113

Reanor, 56

42

Reason, 142
REAVES: Elizabeth, 27
Rebecca, 58, 59, 66, 87, 93, 142, 194, 206, 208
RECTOR: Catherine, 8; Enoch, 154; Harmon, 35; Henry, 22, 23; John, 8, 12, 131; Ludwell, 206; Mary, 8, 23; Nathaniel, 83; Spencer, 43; Thomas, 186, 198; William, 138
REDD: Allen, 93, 95, 185; Joseph B, 191; Joseph B., 179; Joseph Bullett, 41; Permenius B, 185; Prisilla, 41; Susan, 185; Susannah, 41; William J, 185
Redman, 156
REDMON: John, 50
Redmond, 155
REGAN: Lucy, 202
REID: Alexander, 148
REIDS: Samuel, 62
Reiner, 57
Reuben, 16, 18, 20, 22, 27, 38, 44, 45, 52, 56, 63, 66, 68, 76, 81, 83, 85, 90, 95, 99, 103, 105, 106, 110, 116, 117, 121, 122, 123, 125, 130, 131, 133, 141, 144, 145, 146, 147, 151, 153, 157, 163, 167, 170, 174, 181, 188, 197, 200, 201, 202, 206, 208
REUCH: William, 134
Rhoda, 202, 208
Riah, 60, 61
Rial, 143, 148
Rice, 66, 75, 106
Richard, 48, 49, 51, 54, 67, 73, 75, 80, 83, 86, 93, 97, 104, 108, 109, 114, 122, 123, 125, 129, 131, 139, 140, 143, 148, 150, 160, 163, 166, 178, 179, 181, 182, 183, 184, 188, 192, 195, 197, 202, 203

Richard Henry, 108, 114
RICHARDS: Henny, 173; William H, 150
RICHARDSON: Richard P., 115
Richmond, 153
Riley, 138, 158
Ritt, 155
RIXEY: Mary Ann, 151; Richard, 100
RIXEY Jr.: Richard, 79
Riza, 203
ROACH: Thomas, 194, 206
Road, 70
Robbin, 38, 73, 103, 111, 137
Roberson, 200
Robert, 17, 57, 62, 65, 73, 81, 90, 108, 110, 112, 114, 118, 124, 129, 137, 139, 142, 146, 151, 160, 162, 164, 167, 170, 171, 172, 173, 174, 178, 179, 188, 189, 192, 193, 200, 202, 203, 205, 206
Robert Dum, 10
Robert Peyton, 108, 114
ROBERTS: Thomas, 82
Robin, 1, 2, 3, 21, 27, 28, 29, 39, 60, 64, 66, 67, 71, 99, 101, 103, 104, 112, 117, 120, 127, 128, 130, 140, 143, 153, 169, 178, 188
ROBINSON: Benjamin, 29, 31, 46; Diven, 85; Dixon, 29, 133; Elijah, 29, 70; Elisha, 29; George, 29; Henry, 107; James, 29, 80; Jiannah, 54; John, 29; Joseph, 23, 150; Lydda, 29; Martha, 23; Mary, 29; Nathaniel, 29, 177; Sally, 165; Stephen, 29; Susannah, 67, 70; Thomas, 107, 111; William, 85; William C., 164
ROBISON: William C., 138
Roderick, 58, 72, 89, 109

Rodger, 64
Rodgers, 169
Roger, 1, 10, 11, 13, 45, 59, 111, 139
Roger Martin, 45
ROGERS: Ann, 129; Capt George, 186; Edward, 40; George, 40, 204; James, 141; Joanna, 206, 208; Robert, 208
ROGERS Sr.: George, 41
Roll, 172
Rolly, 69, 152
ROOCON: Nancy, 73; William, 73
ROOKARD: Robert, 168; Thomas, 59
ROOKWOOD: Hiram, 163, 183; Nancy, 163, 183; Robert, 163, 183; Thomas, 163, 183
ROPER: Hannah, 119; James, 119
Rosalie, 188
Rosanna, 54
Rose, 7, 9, 17, 23, 27, 28, 30, 31, 33, 35, 36, 37, 38, 44, 45, 46, 47, 50, 51, 53, 55, 58, 59, 60, 64, 65, 66, 72, 74, 76, 77, 78, 79, 80, 83, 84, 85, 89, 93, 94, 95, 97, 100, 101, 104, 108, 114, 116, 118, 119, 122, 123, 126, 137, 140, 144, 145, 148, 149, 153, 155, 158, 173, 174, 178, 179, 184, 192, 193, 195, 206
ROSE: Ann A., 126; Capt. Robert, 110; Mary, 107; Mary S.H., 126, 134, 179; Mary Seymore Hall Allison, 61; Nancy A., 134; Robert, 61, 107, 179, 181; Robert H, 192; Robert H., 134; Robert Henry, 126; William A, 126; William A., 134

Rosel, 65
Rosetta, 142
Ross, 54
ROSSER: George, 149, 153; James N, 187; John, 24; Mary, 11; Priscilla, 76, 149, 153
Roswell, 23
Rosy, 63
ROUSSAU: James, 56; Priscilla, 55; William, 55
ROUTT: Cynthia, 69; Elizabeth, 69, 79, 152; Fanny, 35; Gabriel, 69, 79; James, 47, 69; Peggy, 69; Richard, 84, 88; Synthia, 79; Thomas, 69, 79; William, 69
Roy, 98, 127, 163, 174, 189
ROY: Lydia, 131
Royal, 73
Rozell, 87
RUST: John, 16, 56
Ruth, 27, 123, 125, 153, 183, 188

Sabrey, 128
Sacker, 126
Sal, 3, 4, 22, 31, 57, 60, 61, 85, 111, 134, 166, 200, 205
Sale, 77
Sall, 6, 7, 13, 14, 23, 30, 31, 32, 36, 37, 38, 39, 42, 46, 52, 53, 55, 61, 63, 71, 80, 95, 103, 122, 127, 161
Sally, 17, 35, 41, 42, 49, 53, 61, 62, 64, 65, 66, 69, 72, 77, 82, 85, 92, 93, 97, 98, 99, 100, 105, 108, 109, 110, 111, 112, 113, 114, 117, 119, 122, 123, 125, 127, 129, 133, 144, 145, 147, 148, 149, 153, 154, 157, 159, 160, 162, 164, 166, 168, 169, 170, 174, 175, 178, 179, 188, 193, 195, 200, 201

Sam, 2, 3, 4, 6, 7, 8, 10, 11, 12, 13, 14, 15, 18, 19, 27, 28, 29, 30, 32, 33, 38, 39, 40, 43, 49, 56, 57, 58, 59, 60, 61, 62, 64, 66, 68, 69, 72, 75, 76, 77, 82, 85, 86, 87, 88, 89, 91, 92, 99, 101, 102, 104, 106, 107, 108, 109, 110, 114, 116, 117, 119, 121, 126, 133, 137, 138, 140, 141, 142, 144, 145, 147, 149, 153, 154, 155, 165, 169, 172, 178, 179, 180, 183, 187, 188, 200, 207

Sambo, 9, 12

Sammer, 27

Sammy, 11

Sampson, 11, 15, 36, 37, 38, 42, 66, 73, 74, 93, 97, 112, 127, 163, 169

Samson, 19, 36, 79

Samuel, 7, 8, 17, 31, 44, 54, 56, 62, 74, 79, 81, 83, 94, 99, 130, 145, 158, 159, 164, 174, 193, 197, 201, 207

SAMUEL: Sally, 90; Thomas, 111

Sanders, 162, 173, 191

SANDERS: Ann, 119; Anne, 37; Britain, 119; Elizabeth, 15; Gabriel, 119; James, 15, 119, 170, 177, 187, 189; Judith, 189; Larkin N, 119; Larkin N., 177; Lewis, 119; Mary, 40; Robert, 37, 38, 119; Sally, 147; Sarah, 167; Thomas, 119; William, 190

SANDERS, Sr: James, 195

Sandonia, 188

Sandy, 66, 71, 126, 134, 138, 155, 162, 163, 165, 167, 172, 173, 174, 178, 192, 194, 203, 206, 207

Sanford, 57, 105, 122, 124, 127

SANFORD: Richard, 57

Sapson, 12

Sara, 4, 21, 38, 43, 51, 151

Sarah, 1, 2, 3, 4, 6, 7, 10, 11, 12, 13, 14, 16, 17, 19, 20, 23, 24, 27, 28, 30, 31, 32, 33, 35, 38, 39, 40, 41, 42, 43, 47, 49, 50, 52, 53, 54, 55, 57, 58, 59, 61, 62, 63, 65, 66, 67, 70, 72, 73, 74, 75, 77, 79, 80, 81, 85, 87, 91, 92, 93, 94, 97, 98, 99, 101, 102, 103, 105, 108, 109, 111, 113, 114, 116, 117, 121, 122, 123, 124, 125, 126, 127, 128, 133, 140, 141, 142, 144, 146, 147, 151, 152, 154, 155, 158, 159, 162, 163, 164, 165, 166, 168, 169, 172, 174, 182, 184, 192, 194, 195, 197, 198, 199, 200, 202, 203, 205, 207

Sarah Ann, 190

Sarah Anne, 179

Sarah Jane, 153

Sarah Jones, 1

Sarah Jr., 105

Sarah Mann, 45

Sarah Sr., 105

Sarger, 38

Sary, 50, 57, 86, 88, 90, 149, 156, 163

Saul, 116

Sauncy, 157

Saunday, 110

Saunders, 199

SAURE: John, 8

Savannah, 7

SAWLER: William, 129

Sawney, 20, 67, 68, 73, 128, 143, 144, 148, 186, 204

Sawny, 41

Say, 170

SCANTLANDT: John, 196

SCHUMATE: Daniel, 84; Eliza, 99; Sarah Ann, 84

Scilla, 66, 108, 113, 162

Scillar, 101, 141, 165

45

SHUMATE: Bailey, 29; Daniel, 31; Jane, 118; John, 118, 156, 179; Tabitha, 15; William, 156
SHUMATE Jr.: John, 104
SHUMATE Sr: John, 29
SIAS: John, 19
Sib, 110
Sibba, 147
Sibly, 166
Sickly, 169
Sid, 22, 23
Sidner, 181
Sidney, 142, 150, 158, 174, 193
Siko, 71
Silas, 124, 129, 159
Silla, 11, 37, 92, 114, 179
Sillar, 11, 44, 51, 73, 80, 81, 105, 121, 137, 146, 150
Siller, 11, 24, 103, 106, 108, 137
Silliah, 105
SILMON: Joseph, 161
Silva, 64, 108, 116
Silvanus, 54
Silvey, 183
Silvia, 20, 85, 142, 160, 193
Silvy, 47, 50, 93, 105, 163, 165, 183, 206
Simas, 74
Simms, 188
Simon, 9, 11, 17, 23, 24, 30, 31, 36, 42, 49, 52, 53, 54, 61, 62, 64, 68, 72, 73, 78, 85, 87, 88, 90, 91, 95, 99, 100, 101, 108, 111, 113, 114, 127, 134, 145, 147, 148, 161, 179, 182, 183, 184, 188, 190, 199, 205, 206
SIMPSON: Edward W., 126; Susannah, 117
Sina, 19, 190
Sinah, 10, 32, 72, 105, 117, 118, 119
Sinai, 121, 140, 186

SINCLAIR: Ann, 99; Archibald, 88; Horatio, 104; Horatio John, 88; Isaac, 88, 104; John, 88; Nancy, 88; William, 88, 104, 161
SINCLEAR: John, 7; Robert, 7; William, 7
Sine, 172
Siner, 7, 99, 201
SINGLETON: John, 132; Nancy, 117; Robert, 208
Sinja, 53
SINKLAIR: Lydda, 56; William, 56
SINKLEAR: John, 14; Sarah, 155
Sinry, 110
Sipper, 44
Sirus, 114, 117
Sisley, 29, 32
Skate, 16
SKINKERS: Samuel, 66; Thomas, 66, 68
SLAUGHTER: Juda, 77; Stanton, 77
SMARE: Sarah, 30
Smith, 65, 72, 80, 86, 167, 171, 188
SMITH, 162; Abner, 36, 42, 44, 54; Andrew, 54; Ann, 22; Augusta, 22; Augustine, 22; Benjamin B., 141; Caleb, 79; Calep, 97; Elias, 72; Elijah, 72, 105; Elizabeth, 22, 52, 72, 86, 97, 105, 140, 151; Elizabeth D., 79; Enoch, 72, 73, 105, 155; Enoch D, 203; Hannah, 22, 123; Hedgeman, 105; Hedgman, 72; Isham, 72; James, 22, 87, 165; James W., 109, 165; James Whitacre, 108; Jane, 161; Jas, 189; Jno, 105; Jno., 166; John, 22, 24, 29, 30, 31, 72, 108, 109, 122, 141, 170,

47

180; John B., 125, 140; John M., 141; John P., 109; John Putter, 108; Joseph, 15, 19, 22, 36, 41, 44, 45, 65, 80, 87, 165, 193; Joseph Aldridge, 160; Joseph D, 79; Joseph D., 97; Katherine, 98; Kitty H., 79, 104; Lucinda, 72; Martha, 16; Mary, 30, 69, 86, 89, 160; Matthew, 22, 23, 87; Peggy, 108; Rebecca, 122, 140; Reuben B, 202; Ruth, 36, 42, 44; Solomon B., 140; Susanna, 22; Susannah, 23; Thomas, 22, 52, 140; Walter A., 97; Walter B., 79; Wilhelimina, 45; Wilhilmina, 36; William, 22, 54, 55, 74, 79, 87, 116, 117, 171, 190; William R, 79, 97; William R., 98; Willis G., 165

SODDUST: Mary, 54

Soll, 8

Solomon, 1, 2, 3, 6, 7, 16, 17, 21, 28, 29, 35, 37, 39, 44, 45, 52, 53, 55, 64, 70, 71, 82, 86, 94, 101, 123, 124, 125, 127, 141, 145, 149, 171, 178, 184, 185, 195, 200

Soo, 163

Sook, 7, 38, 124

Sookey, 68, 178, 193, 195, 200

Sophia, 45, 64, 103, 116, 120, 125, 141, 142, 143, 146, 151, 157, 160, 166, 168, 179, 180, 195

Sophy, 192, 200

SPELMAN: Elizabeth, 197; Thomas, 120

Spencer, 3, 44, 59, 62, 64, 68, 72, 74, 79, 80, 87, 88, 90, 92, 94, 97, 100, 103, 107, 110, 111, 120, 125, 132, 140, 147, 149, 155, 156, 172, 178, 184, 188, 207

SPENNY: William, 68

Spico, 93

SPINNY: Benjamin, 67, 68; William, 67, 68

Squire, 185, 190

SQUIRES: Elizabeth, 166; John, 18, 20, 186; Martin, 120, 206

Stacy, 64, 65, 128

STADLER: Jacob, 116, 148

Stafford, 37, 73, 93, 97

STALLARD: David, 139; Hanna, 204

STAMP: William, 8

STAMPS: Mary, 3; Thomas, 3

Stanton, 108

STANTON: William, 78

Stapleton, 108, 114

Staunton, 143, 194

STEATAD: Joseph Bullett, 41; Mary, 41

STEAVING: Nancy, 155

STEELE: George, 170; Henry, 170; John, 170; Samuel, 170, 171, 188; William, 170

STELE: Henry, 105

Stephen, 6, 7, 10, 11, 15, 17, 18, 33, 39, 43, 49, 50, 51, 52, 53, 55, 58, 64, 72, 73, 80, 84, 88, 89, 90, 93, 105, 106, 110, 111, 121, 122, 130, 133, 134, 143, 144, 146, 149, 163, 164, 168, 169, 174, 175, 181, 182, 186, 188, 193, 203, 205

Stephen's Estate, 7

STEPHENS: Robert, 9

Steptoe, 62, 66, 126, 138

STEPTOE: George, 33; John, 33; Joseph, 33

Steven, 72, 89

STEVENS: Alan, 193; Robert, 24; Thomas, 193

STEWART: Allen, 200; Elizabeth, 55, 88, 89, 161; James, 21, 55, 59; Jane, 21; Nancy, 200; William, 21
Stigler: Susanna, 75
STIGLER: Benjamin, 180; Elizabeth, 180; Fanny, 180; George, 180; James, 180; Mildred, 62; Polly, 180; William, 180
Stigler alias CURTIS: Elijah, 75; Elizabeth, 75; John, 75; Lewis, 75; Lucy, 75
STONE: Sarah, 185, 190
STONESTREET: James, 92
STRINGFELLOW: Robert, 121
Strother, 102, 110, 143, 160, 194, 202, 208
STROTHER: James, 17, 199; Jeremiah, 184, 198, 199; John, 199; Lewis, 199; Mary, 199
STURMAN: Foxhall, 81
STYLER: Catherine, 105
Suck, 7, 14, 32, 38, 41, 46, 62, 64, 65, 68, 72, 76, 105, 109, 111, 112, 128, 188
Suckey, 4, 33, 46, 63, 66, 84, 87, 93, 110, 155, 160, 169, 173, 174, 204
Sucky, 31, 64, 65, 109, 125, 141, 151, 153, 163, 170, 178, 194, 202, 204, 205
SUDDETH: Levy, 123
SUDDUTH: Levi, 124, 128, 146; Peggy, 128, 146
Sue, 11, 28, 32, 34, 140
Suk, 44
Sukey, 8, 12, 56, 59, 60, 73, 77, 92, 146, 147, 170, 179, 194
SULLIVAN: Ann, 43; Elizabeth, 43; George, 18, 43; John, 43; Owen, 43
Sully, 133
Summerfield, 194, 197

SUMMERS: Jane E, 201
Summerville, 201
SUNDFORD: Mrs., 100
Susan, 24, 57, 74, 79, 87, 101, 109, 116, 123, 139, 143, 148, 158, 160, 161, 165, 170, 173, 174, 177, 178, 179, 181, 185, 186, 192, 195, 196
Susan Ann, 206
Susanah, 137
Susanna, 10, 13, 32, 41, 80, 120, 123, 171, 204
Susannah, 32, 52, 97, 112, 114, 115, 123, 137, 182, 190, 200
SUTTEL: Sarah, 49
SWANN: Charles, 168
Sybill, 21
Sydney, 159
Sylva, 11, 30, 65, 72, 110, 166
Sylvanius, 62, 77
Sylvia, 10, 70, 81, 85, 100, 116, 133, 160, 172, 174, 180, 194, 195, 200
Synia, 6
Syrus, 137, 139, 154
Sythia, 162

Tabby, 194, 203, 204
Tabitha, 64
Talafara, 178
TALBERT: Ann, 50, 149, 152; Benjamin, 50, 152; John, 50, 52, 152, 166; Paul, 50, 152
Taliafarro, 81
Taliaferro, 32, 160
Tamar, 142
Tamer, 112, 161
Tamson, 75, 77, 159
Tasco, 143
Tayler, 84, 88
Taylor, 109, 118
TAYLOR: Elizabeth, 164; Joseph, 85, 100; Mrs., 100; William F, 147; William I, 106

49

50

Titus, 10, 11, 13, 18, 21, 22, 60, 69, 86, 122, 125, 148, 193, 195

Toanah, 93

Toby, 4, 10, 11, 22, 33, 34, 64, 80, 107, 121, 182, 186

Toliver, 44

Toliver Taner, 82

TOLIVIR: Barnett, 129

TOLLE: Roger, 20; Stephen, 40, 41

Tom, 1, 2, 3, 5, 6, 7, 8, 10, 11, 13, 14, 15, 16, 17, 18, 19, 20, 21, 22, 24, 30, 31, 32, 33, 34, 36, 37, 38, 39, 40, 42, 43, 44, 45, 46, 47, 49, 50, 51, 52, 53, 55, 56, 57, 58, 60, 61, 62, 63, 64, 66, 68, 69, 70, 71, 72, 73, 74, 75, 79, 80, 84, 85, 88, 93, 94, 98, 99, 101, 102, 104, 105, 106, 107, 109, 111, 113, 115, 117, 118, 119, 121, 122, 126, 128, 130, 131, 133, 138, 139, 141, 142, 143, 144, 147, 148, 149, 153, 154, 155, 156, 161, 162, 165, 166, 168, 170, 172, 173, 174, 178, 179, 180, 181, 182, 190, 191, 192, 194, 196, 198, 200, 201, 205

Tom Clayton, 203

Tom Cook, 31

Tom E_tra, 147

Tom Jr., 24, 133

Tom Stones, 61

Tomboy, 22

TOMLIN: John, 51; Mary, 188; Samuel, 51, 170; William, 51

TOMLIN Sr.: John, 51

TOMPKINS: John, 69

Tomson, 205

TONGUE: Cloe, 60, 61; Johnze, 179; Thomas L, 198

Tony, 1, 2, 5, 7, 18, 21, 28, 47, 57, 58, 59, 72, 73, 83, 99, 111, 112, 113, 133, 155, 166, 173, 174

Toring, 166

Toulston, 199

Towmend, 122

Townsend, 91, 148, 184

Towsan, 200

Travers, 180

Travis, 105, 147, 172

Trim, 42

TRIPLETT: Benedick, 45; Betsey, 155; Francis, 45, 46; James, 69; Nancy, 65, 69; Susanna, 155

Troy, 50, 67, 71

True Blue, 102

True Love, 74, 79

Trunk, 133

Tulip, 60, 144, 150, 153, 158

TULLOSS: Alfred, 182; Arthur, 182; Benjamin, 128; Eliza, 182; John I., 128; Nancy, 128; Rodham, 128, 131, 182; Ursula W., 110

TURLEY: Charles, 186; William, 147, 186

TURNBULL: George, 63, 85, 90

Turner, 120, 125, 134, 164, 199

TURNER: Daniel, 123; Edward, 81, 106, 130, 137; Elizabeth, 106; James, 130; John, 123, 125; John M., 123; Mariah, 145; Mary H., 123; Mrs., 185; Samuel, 141

Turtle, 117

TUTT: Elizabeth, 124; John, 206

TYLER: Mary, 4

Ulysses, 109

UNDERWOOD: Mary, 62

UPP: John, 142

Uriah, 88, 205, 206

Uriel, 84, 127

51

Ursuley, 49
URTON: William, 139
Usley, 92
UTTERBACK: William, 184;
  Willis, 202

Valentine, 207
Vall, 70, 92
Venice, 115
Venus, 4, 9, 36, 37, 38, 40, 61,
  66, 68, 78, 83, 89, 90, 93, 97,
  101, 117, 123, 125, 195, 197
Vicentate, 56
Vina, 162
Vinah, 118, 145
Vincent, 103, 158, 174, 181,
  196, 204
Vine, 159, 179
Violet, 11, 12, 19, 20, 24, 29,
  31, 38, 70, 75, 80, 93, 94,
  105, 112, 116, 119, 123, 127,
  128, 133, 134, 144, 145, 146,
  153, 155, 161, 162, 165, 167,
  168, 170, 172, 173, 174, 178,
  187, 188, 194, 198, 201, 205
Virgin, 10, 11, 15, 32, 36, 66,
  205
Virginia, 97, 123, 179, 194
Virlinda, 62
Voltair, 159
VOWLES: Daniel, 196;
  Newton, 196

WADDELL: John, 34, 70
WAITE: Jane, 45; William, 34
WAKE: __ A., 105; Ambrose,
  66
WALLACE: Elizabeth, 131,
  141
WALLER: Betsy, 138; Charles,
  138; John, 47; Mary, 138;
  Prudence, 138; Susanna, 138
WALLERS, 14
Walter, 68
WALTERS: John, 179

Wanger, 193
Wanser, 41, 125, 132
Wansor, 111, 112, 120, 154
Wanzer, 156
WARD: Buckely, 143
Warner, 122
Warrick, 52
Washington, 115, 132, 138,
  153, 160, 162, 170, 181, 185,
  195
Wasner, 200
Wat, 188
Wat Grace, 59, 95
WATERS: Abraham, 141;
  Hannah, 141
Watson, 160
WATSON: Zeperiah, 203
WATTS: Ann, 6; Bennett, 8;
  Francis, 6, 8, 34; John, 8;
  Margaret, 8; Mason, 8;
  Sarah, 91; Thomas, 6, 8
Waugh James, 66
Waulbury, 87
WEATHERBY: Jane, 202
WEATHERS: Cloe, 17; Nancy,
  17
WEAVER: Anne Elizabeth, 1;
  Catherine, 2; Elizabeth, 2,
  164; Eve, 1; Jacob, 2, 99,
  164; James, 99, 119; John, 2,
  164, 170; Martin, 164; Mary,
  164; Shumate N., 164;
  Tilman, 1, 3, 99, 113, 164
WEBB: John, 17; Judith, 17;
  Pressilla, 17; Williamson, 17
WEEDON: Anne, 182;
  Elizabeth, 181; John, 181;
  Rebecca, 182; Thomas W,
  181
WEEKS: Thomas, 167
Weetley, 164
WELCH: Rebecca, 202
WELCH, Sr: Sylvester, 208
Wesley, 98, 178, 179

WEST: Benjamin, 99, 183, 192; Ignatius, 42, 43; James H, 183; Sally, 45; Silas M, 192; William W, 183

Westley, 113, 115, 157, 166, 170, 192

Wh___, 4

WHARTON: Elizabeth, 172; Fanny, 172; George, 172; Isaac, 172; Jemimah, 172; Nelly, 169; Samuel, 105, 147, 172; Silas, 172; Susan, 172; William, 172

WHEAT: Lucy, 56

WHEATLEY: George, 3, 46, 49, 56; Hannah, 155, 158; Heathy, 46; James, 46, 49; John, 46, 49, 97; John J, 84; Joseph, 3, 48, 59; Lauson, 46; Lendon, 46; Mary, 28, 46; Suckey, 46; William, 46, 155

White, 161

WHITE: Ann, 193; James, 94; Mrs., 15; Nancy, 146; William, 84, 172

WHITEFORD: Robert, 77, 93

Whiting, 64, 112, 155, 173, 174

WHITING: Francis, 106, 108, 114; John, 32

WHITLEY: Susannah, 112

WIATT: Conquest, 125, 129; Eleanor, 126

WICKLIFF: David, 49, 116; William, 187

WICKS: Jean, 32

WIGFIELD: Thomas, 130, 131

WIGGINTON: Mary, 59

Wiley, 60

WILEY: Eve, 1

Wilford, 144

Wilfred, 184

Wilkinson, 57

WILKINSON: John W, 185

Will, 1, 2, 3, 4, 5, 6, 7, 9, 10, 11, 12, 13, 16, 20, 21, 23, 24, 27, 28, 30, 31, 32, 33, 35, 36, 37, 38, 39, 41, 42, 43, 45, 47, 48, 49, 50, 51, 52, 53, 56, 57, 58, 59, 60, 61, 62, 64, 66, 68, 70, 71, 72, 75, 80, 82, 87, 93, 97, 99, 103, 104, 106, 108, 111, 113, 114, 117, 126, 127, 134, 143, 147, 150, 159, 160, 168, 169, 174, 175, 177, 179, 193

Will Jr., 80

Will Miller, 66

Willford, 91

William, 2, 3, 28, 41, 44, 51, 52, 53, 59, 62, 64, 66, 74, 79, 93, 97, 104, 105, 108, 112, 114, 123, 125, 128, 131, 133, 137, 139, 140, 142, 143, 144, 145, 147, 150, 151, 153, 155, 157, 158, 159, 160, 162, 163, 164, 166, 167, 169, 170, 172, 173, 174, 177, 178, 179, 181, 184, 186, 188, 189, 192, 194, 195, 197, 202, 207

William H., 173

William Jackson Mathas, 197

WILLIAMS: Ann, 161; Elijah, 126; Elisha, 133; George, 33, 158; Jacob T., 147; John, 24; John Pope, 36; Mary H, 200, 201; Rebecca, 196

WILLIAMSON: Alexander, 77, 80; James, 12

Willis, 32, 36, 37, 46, 50, 60, 62, 63, 69, 73, 74, 75, 77, 79, 88, 90, 93, 94, 97, 101, 102, 108, 114, 122, 126, 127, 137, 140, 143, 163, 165, 178, 179, 191, 192, 194, 202, 203, 205, 206

Willis, 122

Willoby, 31, 71

Willoughby, 24, 28, 62

Willy, 84, 91, 127, 172, 194, 203
Wilobe, 17
Wilson, 48, 125, 156
WILSON: Anne, 83; Eleanor, 131, 133; Henry, 131; John, 172; Nathaniel, 83
Wily, 63
Wina, 81
Windsor, 87, 192
Wine, 38
Winea, 54
WINGGENTON: John W, 185
Winia, 51, 98
Winifred Grace, 95
WINKFIELD: Honor, 58
Winn, 130
WINN: Betty, 45; Eleanor, 117; Hannah, 45; James, 16; John, 16, 117; John W., 124, 126; Mary, 71, 72; Minor, 16, 18, 117, 122, 126, 182; Richard, 16; Thomas, 117, 126; William, 16; Winn, 71
Winna, 33, 40, 88, 93, 143, 204
Winnifred, 5
Winnifred Grace, 59, 97
Winny, 1, 2, 3, 4, 6, 7, 8, 10, 11, 12, 13, 15, 16, 17, 18, 20, 21, 22, 23, 24, 27, 28, 29, 31, 33, 37, 38, 41, 43, 45, 50, 51, 52, 53, 54, 56, 57, 58, 59, 62, 63, 64, 65, 66, 68, 69, 70, 71, 72, 73, 74, 75, 76, 79, 80, 81, 87, 88, 89, 90, 92, 94, 99, 101, 104, 105, 106, 107, 109, 111, 112, 114, 117, 119, 121, 123, 124, 125, 128, 129, 133, 137, 139, 140, 146, 150, 151, 153, 170, 172, 173, 180, 182, 184, 186, 188, 189, 195, 196, 198, 200, 202, 207
Winny Sr., 133
Winson, 23, 163
WINTER: Jacob, 9

WITHERS: Abijah, 47; Augustine, 190; Benjamin, 45; Betty, 75; Chloe, 205; Edward B, 195; Elijah, 75, 162; Elizabeth, 75; Enoch K, 194; Enoch K., 116, 123; Enock, 45; George W., 28; George Washington, 27; Henry H, 195; Horatio C, 195; James, 27, 28, 40, 75, 103, 159, 162, 204, 205; Jamina, 28; Jane M, 195; Jennett, 194; Jennings, 204; Jesse, 75, 149, 162; Jno, 28; John, 27, 45, 75, 204; Joseph, 45; Lewis, 75, 159, 162; Lucinda, 105; Martha, 124; Mary, 162; Mary E, 195; Matthew K., 103; Matthew Keen, 45; Molly, 75; Rose, 42; Spencer, 75, 162; Thomas, 45, 118; Thomas Thornton, 116; William, 28, 45, 75, 77
Wonner, 50
Wonser, 69
WOOD: Dickerson, 72, 74; Elijah, 72; James, 72; Joshua, 117, 119; William, 72
WOODFORD: Catesby, 40, 41; Mary, 40
WOODSIDE: Claryman, 197; Elizabeth, 197; William, 121; William A., 197
WOODWARD: Henley, 84
WOODY: Hedley, 65
WOODYARD: Mendley, 110
Wooter, 163
Worden, 200
Worwick, 53
WRIGHT: Betsey, 39; James, 39; John, 39, 40; Mary, 39, 42, 108, 160; Rosamond, 39, 108, 110; William, 104

WYKOFF: Hannah, 69; Nicholas, 62, 69
Wyne, 74

Yambo, 24
Yarley, 68
Yarrow, 75
YEATMAN: Thomas W, 207; Walker Meredith, 192; Walker W, 184; William T, 184; William Thomas, 192
Yerby, 191
York, 34, 39, 41, 45, 49, 162, 165

YOUNG: Bryan, 39; Eleanor, 112; James, 57, 61; Patience, 39; Peggy, 138; William, 39, 40
Younger, 125
Yourick, 107

Zachariah, 65, 80, 155, 173, 174, 185
Zacharras, 193
Zachary, 38, 53, 60
Zack, 58
Zilpha, 185

56

VOLUME II

WILL BOOKS 11 – 20

1829 – 1847

A. Jack, 32
A. Lucy, 33
Aaron, 10, 32, 34, 35, 46, 51,
  60, 91, 94, 107, 121, 122,
  126
Aaron Mellow, 34
Abagaci, 11
Abarilla, 45, 112
Abba, 29
Abby, 29
Abe, 120
Abedingo, 110, 114
Aberdean, 53
Abigail, 5, 32
Abner, 10, 14, 22, 33, 100, 117,
  120
Abraham, 24, 27, 32, 36, 58,
  60, 65, 66, 67, 68, 106, 117,
  120, 123
Abram, 16, 27, 68, 72, 75, 105,
  118, 121
Absalom, 113
Acinda, 123
Ada, 125
Adaline, 53, 81, 85, 112, 119
Adam, 2, 4, 24, 27, 31, 34, 35,
  51, 52, 54, 57, 63, 66, 68, 75,
  76, 80, 96, 99
ADAMS, 65; B.F., 91;
  Benjamin F., 106; George,
  67; George L., 60; Gustavis,
  126; Hattis, 67; Josiah, 90,
  106; Littleton, 77; Peter, 23;
  Thomas, 23, 25; Thomas M.,
  66; Turner, 14, 30; William,
  21
ADDAM: Thomas M., 89
Addison, 22, 33, 45, 79, 112

Adelaido, 60
Adelia, 19
Adie, 17
Adison, 17, 37
Adley, 111
Adolphus, 18, 98
Agatha, 86, 94
Agga, 10, 45, 73, 77, 83
Aggy, 6, 8, 15, 17, 39, 49, 58,
  59, 60, 61, 64, 68, 88, 107,
  110, 114, 117
Agnes, 7, 8, 22, 36, 114
Ailsey, 90
Alana, 33
Alba, 54
Albert, 16, 18, 38, 39, 60, 63,
  65, 76, 86, 95, 98, 99, 105,
  110, 111, 114, 121
Alcey, 73, 78, 91, 107
Alcinda, 47, 61, 64, 65, 69, 80,
  86, 113, 123
Aleck, 97, 125
Alecy, 78
Aled, 81
Alex, 86, 122
Alexander, 6, 14, 36, 53, 74, 86,
  87, 100, 107
ALEXANDER: Thornton, 24
Aley, 37, 45, 78, 91, 109
Alfred, 1, 2, 3, 4, 5, 6, 8, 10, 14,
  15, 16, 18, 21, 22, 24, 25, 29,
  32, 37, 40, 48, 50, 51, 52, 57,
  60, 61, 62, 65, 68, 73, 75, 76,
  80, 83, 85, 90, 91, 95, 97, 98,
  99, 100, 104, 108, 109, 120,
  121, 125

Alice, 4, 36, 37, 45, 47, 48, 50,
    57, 58, 71, 85, 89, 98, 100,
    107, 112, 118
Alicey, 54
Alick, 34, 99, 102
Allen, 83, 86, 87
ALLEN: Daniel, 17; Mary, 6
ALLISON: William, 77
Ally, 9, 58, 66, 72, 88, 98
Allygany, 68
Alsadia, 37
Alsey, 7, 57, 59, 79
Alvina, 5, 97
Ama, 81
Amanda, 9, 20, 21, 32, 40, 53,
    57, 58, 60, 61, 67, 79, 80, 83,
    86, 98, 99, 114, 124, 125
Amariah, 65
Ambrose, 15, 19, 80, 108
Amelia, 36, 64
America, 107
Amina, 104
Ammoriah, 2
Amos, 48, 54, 109, 111, 117
Ampy, 50
Amy, 7, 19, 22, 36, 41, 53, 58,
    60, 66, 73, 86, 96
Anabella, 10, 42, 51
Ananius, 22
Anderson, 100, 106, 124
Andrew, 36, 39, 50, 54, 64, 84,
    99, 100, 104
Andrew Jackson, 106
Angeline, 29, 30, 34, 68
Angy, 23, 35
Ann, 3, 4, 6, 7, 8, 13, 15, 16,
    18, 19, 23, 24, 25, 32, 33, 35,
    36, 37, 38, 39, 41, 46, 47, 52,
    54, 57, 59, 60, 61, 63, 64, 68,
    71, 76, 78, 80, 83, 84, 86, 88,
    90, 91, 97, 98, 100, 101, 104,
    105, 106, 107, 109, 110, 112,
    113, 114, 121, 122, 124
Ann Eliza, 63, 101, 104, 109,
    125

Ann Maria, 41, 101, 108
Ann Mariah, 75
Ann Marie, 119
Ann Matilda, 51
Ann Richard, 40
Anna, 3, 4, 25, 32, 34, 46, 61,
    63, 65, 75, 88, 95, 102, 107,
    112
Anna Maria, 23, 124
Annabella, 20
Annaca, 25
Annamias, 98
Anne, 107
Anney, 10, 110
Annis, 98
Anthony, 3, 4, 15, 19, 20, 21,
    22, 27, 32, 33, 34, 35, 46, 59,
    75, 76, 85, 96, 99, 103, 110,
    112, 114, 121, 125
Anthy, 124
Anton, 63
Arabella, 26, 35, 66, 73, 77, 83,
    88
Arch, 45, 107, 112, 115
Arche, 100
Archer, 121
ARCHER: Mary, 66
Archibald, 48
Armenia, 108
Armistead, 4, 16, 20, 31, 32, 34,
    40, 58, 64, 65, 75, 87, 90, 91,
    94, 95, 96, 97, 109, 123
ARMISTEAD: Gen. W. K.,
    118; Lewis A, 118; Walker
    K, 117, 118
Armistead Pollard, 101
Arribella, 18
Arthur, 6, 11, 17, 18, 20, 26, 32,
    33, 35, 42, 46, 48, 49, 51, 59,
    60, 64, 66, 71, 73, 75, 78, 80,
    83, 86, 87, 88, 99, 101, 105,
    110, 117, 122
Arthur Locust, 109
Asa, 64

ASH: Ann, 8; Catherine, 8; Francis, 8; Harriet, 8; Maria, 8; Sarepta, 74; Serapta, 81; Thornton, 8
Ashby, 100
ASHBY: Caroline, 45; Caroline M., 57; Clarkson, 36; Elizabeth, 23; Isabella, 45; Issibella McNish, 117; Jno J, 126; John, 31, 45, 62, 86; John H, 30; John H., 39; Martha, 17, 123; Martha T., 45; Nimrod, 9, 14, 30; Roberta, 45; Samuel, 14, 15, 30; Turner, 63; V.T., 113
Ashley, 42
ASHLEY: John, 77
ASHTON: Ann A, 45; Henry W., 113; Sigismunda M., 34
Atwell, 22, 33
Austin, 32, 34, 74, 95, 98, 101
Austin Williams, 109
Ava, 108
Avy, 45
Ayers, 34
AYERS: Charles, 4; Charles W, 29; Charles W., 4, 19
AYRES: Catharine A.W., 58; Catherine A.M., 29; Charles, 11

Backus, 23
BAILEY: Francis, 122; Hannah, 122; Henry, 89, 91, 121; Jane, 122; Letty, 122; Mrs, 122; Nancy, 89, 122
Baker, 110, 114
BAKER: Andrewella, 123; Corbin, 109; Jno, 109; John, 109, 121; John B, 123; Maria, 120, 123; Nancy C, 123; Sophia, 123; William, 120; William Jr, 123
BALDWIN, 125; Elizabeth Turner, 15

BALL: Ann, 115; Benjamin, 84; James, 115; John, 115; Joseph, 115; Lucy Frances, 120; Patty, 99; Sheltial, 115; Shettiel, 2; Taliaferro, 115
BALTHROPE: Dolly, 10; John, 10
BANKHEAD: Ann E., 46; Rosalie L., 58
Barbary, 20
BARBEE: Clair, 61; Clara, 60; John, 49, 53; Mary, 111; Sally, 61; Turner D., 54
BARKER: Lucy, 47
Barnabas, 15, 19
Barnaby, 96, 124
BARNES: Elias, 60
Barnett, 10, 18, 35, 46, 75
BARR: James, 20
Barrett, 7, 20
Bart, 6, 53
Bartlett, 6, 32, 34
Bartley, 94
BASHAW: Robert Hume, 126; Sarah M, 126
BATSON: William, 25
Battaile, 98, 101, 109
Battaile Johnson, 101
BAUIN: Joseph, 46
BAYLESS: Nathaniel B., 25
Bayliss, 80, 123
BAYLISS: Buckner, 40; Martha C, 126; William, 48
BAYLISS Sr.: William, 40
Baylor, 5, 18
BAYLOR: Ann D., 109
BEALE: James A., 60, 84; Richard E, 55; Richard E., 45, 48; William, 31
BEATTY: Ann M., 50
Becky, 58, 67, 117, 118, 125
Becky Withers, 91
Beek, 98
BEEM: Thomas, 23
Beery, 37

Belinda, 46
Bell, 35, 36
BELL: A., 109; Willem, 87
BELT: William, 117
Ben, 4, 5, 10, 14, 16, 17, 18, 19,
    22, 23, 24, 30, 32, 41, 42, 47,
    54, 58, 60, 61, 63, 66, 67, 86,
    89, 91, 98, 99, 103, 108, 110,
    113, 118, 121, 122, 124
Ben Morse, 24
Bene, 99
Benedict, 3, 8, 80
Benjamin, 8, 9, 14, 20, 32, 50,
    53, 68, 73, 93, 97, 111, 115,
    117, 123
Bennett, 110, 114
Berry, 114
BERRY: Thomas Keith, 114
Bertrand, 60
Bet, 6, 38
Betsy, 2, 3, 6, 7, 10, 14, 15, 18,
    19, 20, 22, 23, 27, 30, 33, 35,
    38, 45, 47, 48, 50, 53, 58, 61,
    63, 64, 66, 67, 68, 71, 78, 79,
    83, 85, 90, 91, 95, 96, 101,
    104, 111, 113, 121, 122, 123,
    124
Betsy Scott, 101
Betty, 6, 10, 18, 20, 23, 31, 34,
    36, 39, 47, 48, 49, 51, 54, 58,
    59, 64, 67, 73, 76, 79, 83, 84,
    88, 96, 99, 107, 110, 112,
    114, 119, 121, 122, 125
Betty Jr, 99
Beverly, 16, 32, 34, 36, 71, 73,
    78, 89, 90, 93, 96, 99, 100,
    102, 103, 106, 107, 109, 110,
    114
Beverly Jackson, 101
Beverly Smith, 101
Bill, 6, 10, 14, 22, 23, 26, 30,
    37, 60, 97, 101, 110, 114,
    118, 120, 125
Bill Jones, 60, 61, 109
Bill Nickens, 109

Bill Riley, 101
Billy, 2, 7, 13, 16, 29, 32, 35,
    42, 46, 51, 58, 59, 63, 64, 66,
    73, 75, 77, 78, 79, 80, 82, 83,
    88, 94, 98, 100, 112, 113,
    118, 120
Billy Ash, 126
Billy Blackwell, 99
Billy Keys, 71
Billy Stewart, 10
BISE: Lucelia, 13
BISHOP: James, 103
BLACKSON: Je__, 65
Blackwell, 71, 78
BLACKWELL: Armistead, 59,
    60, 86; Betsy V., 42;
    Elizabeth, 36; Elizabeth P.,
    59; Elizabeth V., 53; Hannah
    R., 21; Jane, 59; Joseph, 22,
    33
BLANKHEAD: Rosalie S., 57
Boatwell, 45
Bob, 4, 10, 15, 16, 18, 23, 24,
    31, 34, 35, 39, 41, 42, 50, 51,
    52, 54, 59, 62, 65, 66, 71, 73,
    76, 77, 83, 85, 86, 87, 88, 91,
    96, 99, 100, 112, 125
Bob Ashton, 85
Bob Sr, 83
Bob Wesley, 85
BOGGESS: Eliza, 86; Maria
    C., 86, 97; Nancy E, 77;
    Rebecca, 5, 18
BOLEN: Jesse C, 108
BOSWELL, 42; James, 108,
    115; Lucy, 108; Lucy A.,
    115; Mrs., 108; William,
    108, 115
BOTCLER: Ann G., 13, 81;
    Joseph, 97
BOWEN: John W., 109;
    William A., 109
BOWIE: George W., 81; John,
    74, 81, 86; Newton S., 81;
    Nimrod S., 81; Watson, 81

BOYCE: Mary C., 50
Bradford, 101
BRADFORD: Benjamin R., 93,
    104; Frances, 95, 105; John,
    93, 94; William Grayson, 65
Brady, 1
BRAHAN: Thomas, 82, 84, 95
BRAUNER: Thomas, 47
BRAY: Lewis, 50, 62;
    Timothy, 50, 62; William
    Franklin, 50
BRENT: Betsy, 37; Willis, 4
BRETT: Nancy, 42
BREWEN, 119
Brian, 47, 81
Bridget, 83, 86, 87
Brister, 85, 86
Bristoe, 32, 34, 100, 105
BRONAUGH: Mary Gray
    Evans, 123
BROOKE: Ann, 15; Francis
    W., 2, 4, 35; Thomas M., 10
Brooks, 75
BROWN: John, 117; Mandly,
    71; Nancy, 117; Thomas, 23
BRUIN: Sarah, 99
Bryant, 64
BRYSONE: Uriah, 57
Buck, 25, 61, 99, 106, 121
BUCKNER: E. Aris, 99; Eliza,
    121; Ella, 99; Ella A, 124;
    Louisa, 121; Louisa B., 99;
    Louisa H., 99; Richard, 76;
    Richard B, 121; Richard B.,
    96, 99; Richard P, 121;
    Richard P., 99
Burgess, 48, 99
BURGESS: Henry, 18
Burke, 15
Burr, 60, 61, 117
Burton, 64, 126
Burtrand, 86
Burwell, 14, 50, 58

Bushrod, 37, 51, 52, 76, 80, 82,
    100, 106, 108, 113, 116, 120,
    123
BUSSEY: Henry, 95
Buster, 20
Butler, 71, 73, 78, 103, 107
BUTTON: Elizabeth, 54; Jane,
    54, 69
BYERATEN: John, 48
BYRNE: Charles, 54; Darby B.,
    36, 38, 54; James, 54; James
    W., 36; Juliet, 38; Juliet
    Ann, 54; Lydia E., 38, 54;
    Uriah, 38, 54; Uriah James,
    38, 54; William, 54

Cadden, 87, 105
Cadden Arthur, 106
Caesar, 10, 34, 50, 59, 64, 95,
    100, 105
Cain, 94, 95
CAITLEGE: Charles, 46
CAITLICH: Charles, 46
Caleb, 119
CALVERT: George, 5, 18
Camilla, 98
Campbell, 98
CAMPBELL: Sarah, 4
Capa Ann, 101
Captain, 101, 109
Carlos, 20
Caroline, 1, 5, 7, 8, 9, 15, 17,
    19, 20, 21, 23, 24, 25, 31, 40,
    45, 46, 48, 49, 51, 52, 54, 60,
    62, 63, 64, 68, 69, 71, 75, 78,
    79, 80, 81, 83, 90, 91, 94, 95,
    97, 98, 100, 104, 107, 112,
    113, 115, 120, 122, 125, 126
CARR: Amanda M., 1, 5, 10;
    Caldwell, 5, 18; John, 1, 6,
    10, 18, 21, 37, 57; Joseph, 5,
    7, 18; Joseph G, 21; Joseph
    G., 7, 40; Peter, 5, 18
Carter, 24, 41, 52, 53, 71, 78,
    79, 80, 101

61

CARTER: Charles L., 73;
Duncan L., 73; Elizabeth, 6,
13, 35; Fitzhugh H., 108;
George, 14, 30, 112, 119;
George Sr, 13; Gustavus A.,
110; H.O.B., 84; Helen, 6;
John, 69, 80; Jonathan, 51;
Judith, 6; Judith F., 6;
Landon, 119; Mary B., 1;
Moon F, 121; Moore F., 6,
53, 80; Moore P., 6; Sarah
Clotilda, 6; Susan C., 73;
Thomas O.B., 104; William
H., 113; William L., 6
CARVER: Bailey, 122; Baily,
126; Frances, 120; Francis,
122; Pamela, 13; Polly, 120;
William, 120, 121, 122
Cash, 119
CASH: John A., 65
Cassa, 68
Cate, 32, 53, 71, 75, 78
Catharine, 5, 57, 119
Catherine, 1, 10, 24, 25, 60, 61,
75, 76, 80, 91, 99, 103, 113,
116, 119, 120, 121, 123, 124,
125
Cato, 15
Caty, 7, 24, 35, 71
Ceasy, 84
Cecelia, 6, 32, 53
Ceila, 6, 112
Ceiley, 119
Cela, 40, 96, 113
Celia, 6, 14, 17, 19, 33, 34, 46,
47, 60, 73, 76, 88, 99, 124,
125
Celin, 85
Cely, 110, 115
Cephas, 48
CHANDLER, 71; Benjamin,
33; Benjamin Lafayette, 49;
Henry J.A., 33; Henry
James, 49; Mary Ann, 33;

Sarah E, 49; Sarah E.A., 33;
William, 49; William A., 33
Chanty, 34
Chapman, 36, 41, 55
CHAPMAN: F.A., 95;
Frederick A, 96; Nathaniel,
54, 72
Charity, 7, 17, 18, 24, 30, 32,
48, 52, 57, 63, 64, 83, 86, 99
Charles, 2, 5, 6, 7, 10, 13, 16,
17, 18, 20, 22, 23, 25, 26, 29,
32, 34, 35, 36, 39, 42, 46, 47,
48, 49, 51, 54, 55, 57, 58, 60,
62, 63, 64, 65, 66, 67, 69, 71,
72, 73, 74, 75, 76, 78, 79, 80,
81, 84, 87, 92, 93, 95, 98, 99,
100, 101, 102, 103, 107, 109,
110, 114, 119, 120, 124, 125,
126
CHARLES: William, 33
Charles Dogins, 84
Charles Henry, 5, 83, 86
Charles Jr., 20
Charles L., 32
Charles Lucus, 34
Charles Pope, 94
Charles Robinson, 101
Charles Simons, 34
Charles Smith, 104
Charles Turner, 123
Charley, 61
Charlotte, 3, 4, 18, 19, 25, 26,
30, 31, 32, 34, 37, 39, 40, 41,
45, 47, 57, 58, 61, 63, 64, 66,
71, 73, 74, 77, 78, 79, 80, 85,
89, 91, 94, 98, 99, 103, 104,
105, 109, 112, 113, 115, 119,
120, 121, 122, 123, 125
Charlotte Glascock, 42
Charni, 38
CHICHESTER: Richard
McCarty, 5
CHILD: Margaret, 17; Robert
A, 120
Chilton, 5, 7

CHILTON: David, 62;
  Elizabeth, 61; Henrietta, 62;
  Maria, 15; Maria R., 62;
  William O, 69; William O.,
  80
China, 104
CHINN: C.E., 107; Charles,
  107, 108
Chloe, 3, 4, 35, 49, 59, 77, 85,
  91, 99, 110
Chloe Elizabeth, 99
Chris, 61
Christian, 80
Christopher, 65, 73, 85
CHUNN: Andrew, 15, 120,
  123; Andrew I, 123; Ann M.,
  93; C.E., 104; Capt., 93;
  Charles P., 104; Elijah, 104;
  James Thomas, 123; Jno M.,
  91; John F., 104; John M,
  120; John M., 76, 82, 93,
  113, 116; Lucinda E., 104;
  Lucy M., 116; Martha, 14,
  29, 30, 39, 42; Mary C., 116;
  Sarah W., 116; William S,
  123; Zachariah T, 123
Cillar, 17, 41, 52, 102, 106
CLANAHAN: William M., 97
Clancy, 65
Clara, 5, 7, 14, 21, 34, 37, 40,
  95, 96, 98, 100, 111, 117,
  119
Clarissa, 13, 14, 45, 98, 110,
  112, 114
Clarisy, 9
CLARK: John H., 57;
  Lusianna, 59; Mary Ann, 47,
  51, 67; Thomas, 33, 59
CLARKE: Joel, 16; John H.,
  32; Mary Ann, 37, 62;
  Richard, 16; Thomas, 16, 18
CLARKSON: Marion, 65;
  William, 65
Clary, 3, 6, 7, 9, 25, 54, 57, 93
Clayton, 20

Cleo, 51
Cloe, 69, 112, 114, 121, 122
CLOPTON: Alford, 108;
  Alfred, 115; Doc., 108; John,
  115; N.V., 115; Sally, 108;
  William, 108
Cluny, 15
COCKE: Elizabeth, 3
Coe, 38
Colbert, 61
Coleman, 35
COLEMAN: Samuel, 89
Coley, 81
Colt, 119
Columbia, 101
COLVIN: George, 23;
  Haywood, 23; James, 23;
  Lawson, 23; Lydia, 23;
  Richard, 23; Sarah, 23;
  William, 23
COMBS: May Seth, 39; Robert,
  96; Sally, 35, 53
Comfort, 63
Commadore, 99, 103
Coniled, 67
Conner, 110, 114
CONNER: Hannah, 74; Mirah,
  84
Connor: W., 1
CONWAY: Peter, 29, 42
Cook, 99
COOK: Nancy, 31; Philip, 77;
  Washington, 48
COOKE: Kemp F., 80, 91
COOPER: John, 47
Cora, 87, 98, 105, 106
Cordelia, 101
CORDER: Nathan, 68
Corker, 93
CORLEY: Jane, 116; Manoah,
  116
Cornelia, 87, 115, 122, 125
Cornelius, 40, 101
CORNELL: Silas, 81; Syntha,
  81

CORNWALL: Jacob, 16
COWNE: Susan, 13; Susan
   Ann, 13
COX: Harriet, 105; James, 83,
   84, 89; John, 84; Samuel, 84;
   Whitson, 84
Coy, 110
Craig, 58
CRAIN: Capt. John, 80; Jas, 80;
   John, 62
CRAINE: John, 2, 3, 8, 37, 48,
   81; Molly, 2; Sally, 2, 8
Crandford, 25
Cravin, 47
Crawford, 20
Crib, 115
Crissy, 63
Crissy Jane, 109
CROPP: Richard, 8
CRUMP: Ellen, 6; Francis, 6;
   James Addison, 6; Kitty, 6;
   Lucinda, 6; Lucy, 6; Nancy,
   3; William, 6
CRUPPER: John, 58, 81, 82;
   Winefred, 81
Cry, 115
CULVERHOUSE: Elizabeth,
   76, 77
Cupid, 22, 59
Curry, 95
CURTIS: Mary, 17
Cynth, 42
Cynthia, 14, 50, 98
Cynthy, 49
Cyrus, 32, 36, 38, 42, 49, 93,
   96, 105, 112, 118, 120
Cytha, 64

Daisy, 14
Dalilah, 101
Dangerfield, 16, 74, 101, 103
Dangerfield Mason, 109
Daniel, 3, 4, 5, 6, 8, 9, 10, 11,
   13, 14, 16, 17, 23, 24, 25, 27,
   31, 36, 37, 42, 45, 47, 48, 49,

50, 51, 52, 57, 58, 60, 62, 63,
   64, 65, 66, 67, 69, 71, 73, 78,
   80, 81, 83, 86, 87, 94, 95, 98,
   100, 101, 106, 110, 111, 113,
   114, 115, 119, 120, 121, 123
DANIEL: H.D., 62; Henry JM,
   118
Daniel Jr., 3, 8, 95
Daniel Sr., 95
Danis, 37
Daphne, 6, 26, 124
Darkey, 14, 35, 125
Dave, 126
DAVERSON: Theo, 80
David, 8, 15, 34, 35, 36, 37, 39,
   57, 64, 71, 73, 75, 97, 104,
   108
David Henry, 109
DAVIS: John C, 39; John C.,
   11; Mary, 57; Sidney G., 39;
   Thomas, 46
Davis Brigo, 11
Davy, 3, 8, 10, 32, 46, 54, 55,
   62, 65, 69, 81, 94, 99, 101,
   109, 118
DAWES: Eliza F, 63; Eliza F.,
   59; James E, 68; James E.,
   59; Mary A.M., 59, 68
Dawson, 104
DAWSON: Bradford, 61
DEAR: Sally Ann, 111
DEERING: William R, 76
Delfa, 10
Delia, 5, 8, 15, 16, 24, 25, 33,
   40, 57, 60, 65, 71, 75, 83
Delilah, 14, 45, 73, 110
Delphia, 15, 19, 52
DENEALE: William, 68
Dennis, 2, 6, 13, 18, 32, 33, 34,
   39, 40, 67
Dennis Napper, 101, 109
Dennis Payton, 101
DENT: Col. William, 93
Diana, 45, 112, 115

64

Dick, 1, 2, 4, 7, 17, 20, 21, 22, 24, 27, 32, 34, 41, 54, 60, 61, 64, 67, 68, 71, 72, 75, 79, 95, 98, 99, 100, 106
Dick Page, 34
Dicy, 23
DIGGS: Ann C., 35; Catherine L., 35; Edward, 107; Elias West, 35; Elizabeth, 35; Georgeanna B., 87; John B., 35; Ludwell, 52, 85; Porcia, 87, 105, 106; Porcia M.L., 87; Sarah L., 52; Sarah P., 35; William H., 35; William Henry, 35
Diley, 107
Dilly, 14, 62
Dinah, 2, 6, 15, 19, 33, 36, 39, 41, 55, 61, 63, 91, 94, 99, 103, 105, 108, 110, 114
Diner, 11, 65, 110
Dino, 86
DIXON: Alex, 64; Alexander, 19, 26, 34, 49, 59; Alice, 11, 19, 26, 34, 64; Charles, 19, 26, 34, 64; Charles C., 19, 26, 50; Edward, 64; George B., 50, 64; Henry, 118; Henry I., 64; John, 19, 26, 34, 50, 64, 100; Lucicous, 59; Lucius, 19, 26, 34, 50, 64; Maria, 11, 26, 30; Mariah, 64; Turner, 64; William, 20, 25
Dizza, 68
Doc Henderson, 121, 122
DODD: Ann, 20, 21, 22, 24, 41; Benjamin, 25; Sanford, 30; Sarah Agnes, 41; Stephen, 61; William, 25
Dolly, 3, 8, 9, 15, 45, 58, 63, 68, 76, 77, 97, 104, 121
Dolly Ann, 68
Donmey, 66
Dorcus, 98

Douglas, 32, 34
DOWELL: Anna, 125; Catharine Elizabeth, 38; Elisha, 125; Julia A., 38; William F, 126
DOWNES: Henry, 46
DRUMMOND: Aaron, 50, 62, 76, 84, 86; Leannah, 84; Nancy, 84, 106
Drusilla, 104, 109
Dudley, 18, 101
Duff, 95
DULANY: Mrs., 63
Dulcena, 52
DUVALL: Sarah, 13

Eady, 49, 60
Easter, 6, 48, 97, 112, 115
Easter Simpson, 101
EASTHAW: George, 8
Eda, 75
Edie, 39, 46, 53, 90, 91, 97
Edinburgh, 7, 21
Edith, 41, 68, 94
Edmond, 1, 2, 4, 5, 7, 8, 13, 14, 17, 24, 32, 57, 63, 78, 117
EDMOND: Naomi, 65
EDMONDS: A.T., 104; Alacie T., 104; Alice T., 101, 104; Col. Elias, 41; Elias, 36; Frances, 36; Francis, 55; John, 2; Lewis, 36; Margaret, 104; Margaret B., 100, 101, 104; Mary Evelina, 6; Sarah B., 30; Thomas W., 109; William F., 6
Edmonia, 80, 101
Edmund, 10, 23, 25, 34, 35, 53, 80, 104, 110, 114
Edna, 106
Edward, 5, 6, 13, 20, 23, 36, 50, 64, 65, 75, 76, 100, 104, 108, 116, 117, 120, 121, 123

EDWARDS: Basil, 72; Elijah,
52, 72; Elizabeth, 72; H.W.,
72
Edwin, 71, 73, 78, 90, 93, 103
Edy, 97
Egbert, 51
Eland, 119
Eleanor, 72
Elender, 60
Eleven, 99
ELGIN: Catherine, 32;
Elizabeth, 32; Jesse, 25;
Lucy, 25; Phebe, 51
Eli, 10, 11, 15, 25, 67, 74, 86,
125, 126
Elias, 9, 11, 14, 18, 20, 21, 24,
26, 27, 35, 36, 38, 42, 51, 55,
59, 60, 62, 66, 73, 89, 94, 99,
111, 114
Elick, 119
Elijah, 5, 18, 24, 25, 31, 63, 69,
101, 115
Elijah Locust, 109
Elijah Whitfield, 32
Elisa, 4, 31, 37, 115, 119
Elisha, 31, 32, 34, 98
Eliza, 3, 4, 5, 6, 7, 8, 9, 10, 14,
15, 17, 19, 22, 24, 26, 29, 32,
34, 38, 42, 45, 46, 51, 53, 54,
57, 58, 60, 61, 62, 67, 71, 73,
77, 78, 79, 80, 85, 86, 89, 90,
91, 94, 98, 100, 101, 104,
105, 107, 109, 110, 112, 113,
120, 121, 123
Eliza Jr., 4
Elizabeth, 4, 10, 18, 20, 21, 38,
45, 46, 54, 58, 62, 67, 75, 80,
98, 101, 104, 107, 110, 112,
114, 119, 124, 125
Elizy, 75
Ellen, 4, 17, 19, 20, 23, 31, 33,
37, 38, 45, 46, 50, 54, 57, 60,
61, 62, 63, 66, 67, 68, 71, 73,
75, 76, 78, 79, 80, 83, 84, 86,

95, 98, 99, 102, 105, 106,
120
Ellick, 41, 55, 71, 123
Ellinda, 97
Ellis, 14
ELLIS: Lewis, 119; William,
115
Elly, 65
Ellzey, 62, 63, 68, 72, 74
Elmira, 96
Elon, 16, 18
Elser, 103
Elvia, 101
Elvira, 109
Ely, 19
Emaline, 10, 48, 99
Emancipated: Aggy, 68; Ann,
68; Anna Maria, 124; Becky
Withers, 91; Betty, 88; Betty
PARKER, 68; Charles, 69;
Clara, 111, 117; Dick, 68;
Edmond, 117; Elizabeth, 68;
Emma, 88; Fanny Warner,
68; Fleet, 88; George, 94;
George Warner, 68; Hannah,
117; Henry, 68; Henry
Warner, 68; Jack, 94; James
Warner, 68; Jane, 88; John,
88; Lewis Warner, 68;
Linsey, 88; Lucy, 100; Lucy
Malvin, 91; Mary, 68; Ned,
100; Parker Warner, 68;
Perry, 68; Richard, 68;
Robin, 69; Sam Withers, 91;
Scirus, 69; Thornton
Withers, 91; Tully, 117;
Warner, 100; William, 65;
Willis, 117; Winny, 69
Emanuel, 1, 2, 52, 123
EMBREY: William, 1
EMBRY: Thomas, 31
Emiline, 60, 98
Emily, 3, 4, 15, 16, 18, 21, 23,
24, 27, 30, 31, 38, 45, 47, 49,
60, 62, 63, 71, 73, 84, 86, 94,

98, 99, 106, 113, 115, 123, 125
Emma, 33, 46, 57, 64, 88, 105, 106, 115
EMMONS: Daniel, 119; James, 78, 85, 119; Mary, 78, 85
Emmy, 5, 75
Emond, 8
Emrey, 63
ENGLISH: Anna Maria, 105; James, 33
Enoch, 3, 7, 9, 20, 31, 33, 34, 39, 47, 49, 54, 57, 59, 95, 98, 99, 101
Enoch Mason, 109
Enos, 81
Ensey, 50
Ephraim, 14, 46, 80, 101
Ephran Hall, 32
Esau, 8, 52, 57, 110, 115
ESKRIDGE: Emily Ann, 89; Harriet, 89; Isa Matilday, 89; James, 89; Jane, 31; M., 85; Samuel, 31, 34, 52, 68, 105
Esom, 3
Essex, 36
Esther, 15, 41, 48, 61, 64, 75, 80, 98, 101, 103, 110
Eugene, 42, 57
Eugenia, 98
EUSTACE: Isaac, 13, 15, 75, 81; Isaac Lee, 13, 81; John, 75; Susan, 13, 81; William, 13, 81
Evalina, 110
Evaline, 71
Evan, 25
Evans, 118
EVANS: Mary G., 95; Susan, 95
Eve, 7, 41, 90, 93, 94, 103, 111, 124, 125
Evelina, 1, 5, 8, 14, 16, 24, 37, 39, 48, 52, 57, 58, 59, 62, 63,

64, 79, 83, 86, 87, 91, 97, 98, 100, 114
Eveline, 21, 31, 38, 40, 45, 83, 114
EVENS: Elisha B, 95; Elisha B., 96

Fan, 104, 119
Fanny, 2, 4, 5, 6, 7, 9, 10, 15, 16, 17, 18, 19, 24, 25, 26, 32, 34, 35, 37, 38, 41, 46, 47, 50, 52, 57, 58, 60, 61, 62, 63, 64, 65, 66, 71, 75, 77, 78, 79, 80, 83, 86, 87, 90, 93, 94, 95, 96, 98, 99, 100, 101, 104, 106, 107, 108, 109, 110, 112, 113, 114, 118, 119, 121, 124, 125
Fanny Warner, 68
FANT: John S., 97; Joseph N., 104; Margaret, 95
Farley, 110
FARROW: Dolly, 95; Lucy, 71; Sally, 94
Fay, 21
FEAGAN: Richardson, 69
Fedelia, 32
Felicia, 4, 15, 73
Fenton, 18, 19, 85, 96
FERGUSON: James, 108; Thomas, 108, 124
Festus, 60, 86
FICKLIN: A.S., 106; Ann C., 62; Anthony S, 121; Charles, 31, 41, 42; Frances M., 104, 107; Gustavus L., 103; Lewis, 74, 103; Mary, 42; WP, 103
FICKLIN Jr.: Charles B., 31
FIELD: Hannah, 107; Joesph, 78; Joseph, 119; William D, 119
Fielding, 14, 45, 73, 76
FIELDS: Hannah, 105
FISHBACK: Amanda, 11, 25, 47, 81; Ann, 11, 25, 81;

Frederich, 38, 122
Frederick, 2, 18, 23, 24, 33, 60,
    75, 86, 91, 95, 97, 107
Fredrick, 7
FREEMAN: James, 74; Sarah,
    74; William, 33; William C.,
    1
French, 17
FRENCH: Alpheus, 36
Fullus, 75
FULTON: Mary, 105; William,
    105
FURR: Jackson, 93

Gab, 7
Gabriel, 8, 14, 20, 23, 45, 66,
    91, 95, 123
Gaines, 57
GAINES: John, 91; Seth, 36
GAINS: Elender, 68
Garland, 95
Garner, 80
GARNER: James, 112; John,
    90, 97, 106
GASKINS: Alfred, 113; Henry,
    124
Genge Annah, 66
George, 4, 5, 6, 7, 8, 10, 13, 14,
    15, 16, 17, 18, 19, 20, 21, 22,
    23, 24, 31, 32, 33, 34, 35, 36,
    37, 39, 40, 41, 45, 46, 47, 48,
    49, 51, 52, 53, 54, 58, 60, 61,
    62, 63, 64, 65, 67, 69, 71, 72,
    73, 74, 75, 76, 77, 79, 80, 81,
    84, 86, 90, 91, 93, 94, 95, 97,
    98, Ï99, 100, 102, 103, 104,
    105, 106, 107, 109, 110, 111,
    112, 113, 115, 117, 119, 120,
    121, 122, 123, 124, 125, 126
GEORGE: Benjamin, 72
George Ann, 75
George Gaines, 101
George Henry, 35, 76
George Henry Lucas, 57
George Jr., 5, 95, 104

George Sr., 104
George Strother, 41
George W., 39
George Washington, 76
George William, 101
George Willis, 107, 109
George Winters, 101, 109
Georgeanne, 94
Georgiana, 109
Georgy, 63
Gerard, 15, 19, 23, 85
Gibson, 126
GIBSON: John, 91; Thomas, 42
Gilbert, 64
Giles, 36, 57
Gilman, 25
Gilson, 46
Ginny, 6
Ginny Traverse, 89
GLASCOCK: Aaron, 9;
    Addison, 10; Daniel, 4, 60;
    David O., 62; Enoch, 119;
    Hannah, 103, 119; Henry,
    68; Hezekiah, 99, 103, 119;
    James D., 61; John, 108;
    Joseph, 9; Marie, 103; Mary,
    37; Nancy, 35, 61; Peter, 2;
    Thomas, 1, 9; Thomas I., 62;
    Thomas W., 61; Uriel, 51;
    William, 108
GORE: Nancy, 108, 109
Gowin, 41, 89
Grace, 6, 14, 17, 25, 30, 32, 34,
    39, 53, 94, 98, 99, 104, 108,
    115
Gracy, 124
Gracy Jr, 124
Gradison, 36
GRAHAM: Peter, 1
Grandison, 24, 51, 52
Grant, 99
GRANT: John, 49
GRAY: Thomas, 82, 95
GREEN: Ann, 65; Chapman,
    36; Charles, 36; Elizabeth,

69

11; Hugh R., 111, 113;
James S., 24; John, 22, 36,
37, 38; Mrs., 88
Greenberry, 95
GRIBY: William G., 36
Griffin, 21
GRIFFIN: Lourinda S., 88
GRIFFITH: Elijah, 99, 102;
Evan, 99; John, 99
GRIGSBY: A.S., 40; Nathaniel,
48; Sally, 100; Thornton,
110; William, 33; William
G., 36
GUNYON: Capt. William, 50;
Mary, 32; William, 32, 47
Gus, 101, 106, 124
Gustavus, 1, 4, 18, 20, 73, 77,
79, 93
Gusty, 63
Gwinn, 30, 32
Gwyn, 34

Haden, 68
Hagar, 57
HALE: Francis, 34, 35; Francis
P., 16, 37; Francis T., 62;
Mrs. E., 62; William, 94
Hampshire, 7
HAMPTON: F., 35; John, 51
HAND: Absalom, 54
Hanford, 7
Hanibleton, 111
Hanna, 64
Hannah, 1, 8, 10, 11, 14, 15, 17,
18, 19, 20, 22, 24, 25, 27, 31,
34, 38, 39, 40, 41, 45, 46, 47,
48, 49, 50, 52, 53, 54, 57, 60,
63, 64, 66, 67, 68, 71, 73, 74,
75, 76, 82, 83, 84, 85, 86, 87,
89, 91, 94, 95, 98, 99, 103,
104, 107, 108, 110, 113, 117,
121, 122, 124, 125
Hanner, 8
Hannibal, 36, 94, 98
Hanover, 110

HANSBROUGH, 24
Hansford, 5, 21, 40
Hanson, 3, 115
HARDING: John, 106; John B,
118
Hardwick, 57
HARRELL: Sarah Jane, 89;
Susan Jackson, 89
Harriet, 4, 6, 7, 8, 13, 14, 16,
17, 18, 21, 22, 23, 24, 25, 30,
31, 34, 37, 39, 40, 42, 45, 46,
47, 48, 52, 53, 54, 58, 60, 61,
62, 63, 64, 65, 66, 68, 69, 71,
73, 75, 76, 78, 80, 83, 84, 85,
86, 91, 93, 94, 97, 98, 99,
100, 101, 104, 107, 108, 110,
112, 113, 115, 120, 121, 122,
123, 124, 126
Harriet Blackwell, 16
Harriet Gibson, 109
Harriet Jones, 16
Harriet Lucy, 32
Harris, 11, 39
HARRIS: James W, 122;
Thomas, 96
Harrison, 30, 31, 49, 54, 73, 79,
80, 100, 120, 123
HARRISON, 78; Benjamin,
125; Daniel B, 125; Leonora,
125
Harry, 3, 4, 6, 7, 8, 9, 11, 14,
19, 20, 23, 24, 30, 32, 34, 36,
37, 42, 45, 46, 47, 51, 60, 62,
64, 67, 69, 73, 80, 88, 95, 96,
100, 101, 107, 112, 117, 120,
125
Harry Skinner, 22
HART: Robert, 45
Hartley, 98
Harwich, 123
Haunton, 20
Hauson, 36
HAYES: Mrs., 48; Nancy, 47,
111
HAYNIE: Martha H, 126

Headly, 18
Helen, 6, 65, 95, 99, 100, 101, 104
HELENUS: Benjamin, 100
HELFIN: William, 109
Hemburn, 115
Hend, 88
Henderson, 75
HENDERSON: Richard H., 54
Henley, 19, 45, 48, 74, 84, 86
Henny, 9, 25, 27, 45, 48
Henrietta, 9, 57, 74, 91, 97, 98, 107, 125
Henry, 1, 4, 5, 6, 8, 10, 14, 15, 16, 17, 18, 20, 22, 23, 24, 25, 29, 30, 31, 32, 34, 35, 36, 37, 39, 40, 41, 42, 46, 47, 51, 52, 53, 55, 58, 61, 63, 64, 65, 66, 67, 68, 71, 72, 73, 74, 75, 76, 77, 78, 80, 81, 82, 84, 85, 88, 90, 91, 93, 94, 95, 96, 98, 99, 100, 101, 102, 103, 104, 105, 107, 108, 109, 110, 111, 112, 113, 114, 115, 116, 117, 118, 120, 121, 123, 124, 125
Henry Clay, 104, 107, 110, 114
Henry Fitzhugh, 101
Henry Jr., 10, 124
Henry Lewis, 101
Henry Lock Mann, 5
Henry Moore, 109
Henry Smith, 57
Henry Toler, 32
Henry Wansee, 42
Henry Wilson, 14
Henson, 3, 4, 9, 39, 57, 59, 117, 118
Hepsy, 120
Hercules, 86, 87
HEREFORD: Francis, 8, 21; Nancy, 120, 123; William A, 120
Herman, 87, 105, 106
Hester, 74, 95, 98

HICKERSON: Ann, 31; Betsy, 31; Daniel, 18, 31; John H, 126; John H., 31; Mrs., 22; William E., 31
HICKS: Ann Matilda, 100; Benjamin, 100; Emma, 35, 51, 100; Emma E., 100; Isaiah A., 100; Kimble, 64; Mary, 100; Stephen, 37, 100; Stephen G., 100; Thomas K., 100
Hill, 53
HILL: Jesse E., 39; Pitman C., 39; Tersissa F., 39
HINSON: George, 109
Hisham, 38
HITCH: Burgess, 49; Elizabeth, 23; John, 23; Lizzy, 23; Turman, 23; William, 23; William M., 32
HITT: Mary Catherine, 83; Peter, 62
HIXSON: Amanda, 76; Amanda L., 114
HOLLINGWAY: Charles, 67
HOLLOWAY: George, 68, 69; Susannah, 68
HOLM: Frances, 23
HOLMES: Catherine Ann, 89; Margaret George, 89
HOLTZCLAW: Climent, 38; Eli, 106
HOMES: Mary Ann T., 100
HOPPER: Mary, 89, 94
Horace, 41, 54, 60, 73, 94, 95, 101, 109, 119, 123
HORD: Ambrose, 74; Catherine M., 46; Catherine Matilda, 46; Charity, 74; Enos, 74; William, 74
HORNER: Mary A.T., 106; Mary Ann, 67
HORTON: Craven, 53
Housen, 95
Howard, 27, 63

HUDNALL, 60
HUGHS: Thomas, 71
Hulda, 1, 5, 10, 20, 21, 37, 53,
    97, 102, 122
Huldy, 7
HUME: Col. Asa, 48; Jacob,
    126; Jane, 126; John Robert,
    126
Humphrey, 4, 38, 126
Humphry, 126
Hunter, 38
HUNTON: Charles, 63, 107;
    Eppa, 8, 22, 33, 71; Gen.
    Thomas, 1, 20; John, 20, 35;
    John B, 51; John B., 10, 18,
    26, 42, 59, 66, 73, 77, 83,
    88; John H, 118; Maj.
    Charles, 47; Matilda, 20;
    Robert, 18; Robert H., 11,
    26, 35, 42, 51, 59, 66, 73, 78,
    83, 88, 100; Robert Henry,
    20; Sarah L., 54; Sarah
    Lucelia, 20, 53; Thomas E.,
    54; Thomas Edward, 20;
    William, 69, 73
HURONALL: James, 7;
    William, 7
HURST: Thompson M., 106
Huson, 51
HUTCHINSON: Alexander,
    67; Kitty, 35, 51; Samuel,
    51; Susan, 98
HUTCHISON: Alexander, 122;
    Cornelia, 122; Cynthia, 122;
    Edgar, 122; Maria, 122;
    Reuben, 122
Hyram, 91

Ian, 99
Idea, 7, 22
Imman, 26, 101
Ines, 124
INGRAM: Lucy, 15
INGRHAM: Thomas B.P., 15
IOH: George H., 108

Isaac, 4, 5, 10, 13, 14, 20, 71,
    73, 78, 83, 88, 89, 90, 95, 96,
    99, 103, 110, 112, 115, 120,
    123, 125
Isabel, 15, 19, 83, 96, 110, 115
Isabella, 65, 86, 96, 123, 124,
    125
Isaiah, 112
ISH: William K., 46
Isham, 115
Ismar, 63
Israel, 29, 39, 80, 113, 121, 122
Issac, 34
Ivan, 48

Jack, 5, 6, 8, 10, 13, 14, 15, 18,
    19, 20, 22, 23, 24, 30, 31, 32,
    34, 37, 39, 40, 41, 47, 48, 57,
    63, 64, 66, 67, 71, 72, 73, 78,
    79, 81, 85, 86, 88, 90, 94, 96,
    97, 98, 99, 103, 107, 108,
    110, 111, 112, 113, 114, 118,
    120, 123, 124, 126
Jack Ashton, 58, 66, 72
Jack Thompson Mann, 5
Jackson, 30, 39, 47, 48, 63, 69,
    80, 90, 97, 98, 101, 121
Jacob, 30, 36, 40, 46, 47, 58,
    64, 66, 68, 79, 80, 91, 94,
    108, 110, 121, 122, 123, 125
Jake, 1
Jambella, 95
James, 1, 3, 5, 6, 7, 9, 15, 16,
    17, 19, 20, 21, 22, 23, 24, 25,
    27, 29, 30, 31, 32, 34, 36, 37,
    40, 41, 42, 45, 50, 51, 53, 57,
    58, 61, 62, 63, 66, 68, 71, 72,
    73, 75, 77, 78, 79, 80, 86, 91,
    92, 94, 95, 96, 98, 100, 101,
    104, 108, 110, 112, 113, 117,
    119, 120, 121, 122, 124, 125
JAMES: David, 123; Delia, 40;
    Duncan, 123; Edwin, 123;
    Elizabeth, 40; James C., 90,
    93; Maj. D., 80; Martha S.,

90; Sally, 123; Susan, 123;
Waverly, 123
James (Scoggins), 39
James Hunter, 109
James Marshall, 101
Jamima, 38
JAMISON: Ann, 41
Jamma, 60
Jane, 4, 5, 6, 7, 8, 11, 13, 14,
15, 18, 19, 20, 21, 22, 24, 25,
30, 31, 34, 35, 37, 38, 39, 40,
41, 42, 45, 49, 50, 51, 53, 54,
57, 58, 59, 60, 61, 62, 63, 66,
67, 68, 71, 73, 76, 78, 80, 81,
83, 85, 88, 90, 91, 96, 97, 98,
99, 100, 101, 102, 104, 108,
110, 112, 114, 117, 121, 123,
125
Jane Arabella, 23
Jane Winters, 109
Janet, 27, 30, 52, 64, 119
Janey, 71, 72
Janny, 2, 8, 10, 16, 18, 23, 37,
57, 97, 101
Jaqulin, 113
Jared, 41, 125
Jarissa, 95
Jarrett, 80, 96, 103
Jarrot, 119
Jas William, 98
Jeadora, 57
Jeannah, 15, 24, 124
Jeff, 123
Jefferson, 4, 7, 52, 57
Jeffrey, 5, 14, 25, 67, 77
JEFFRIES: Alex, 102;
Alexander, 106; Eli, 106;
Enoch, 36, 38, 51, 104;
George, 18; James, 36; Jno,
106; John, 36, 106; Joseph,
36; Moses, 106
Jemima, 40, 41, 45, 52, 67, 75,
107
Jemimy, 21, 23, 39, 67
Jemina, 17

JENKINS, 119; W.M., 113
Jennet, 123
JENNINGS: Alfred C., 112;
Augustine, 10; Austin, 112;
Carola, 15; Carola G.A., 45,
112; Edwin D, 125;
Elizabeth JW, 125; Fenesca
B., 15; J L F, 125; John, 35;
Lewis, 15, 19, 96, 113, 124;
Lewis A., 112; Lucinda A.,
15; Lucy B., 112; Margaret,
15, 96; William H., 46
Jenny, 4, 7, 13, 15, 22, 23, 24,
33, 37, 41, 45, 46, 47, 48, 49,
52, 54, 60, 65, 67, 71, 78, 84,
85, 102, 106, 108, 114
Jerard, 26, 74, 96
Jeremiah, 15, 19, 47, 122
Jerrett, 77, 85
Jerry, 1, 17, 22, 24, 31, 33, 39,
45, 52, 62, 63, 80, 98, 100,
110, 112, 114, 115, 124
Jess, 48, 60
Jesse, 1, 7, 8, 10, 14, 17, 30, 32,
36, 37, 48, 50, 58, 59, 64, 67,
71, 72, 84, 96, 97, 98, 104,
107, 109, 110, 112, 115, 117,
123, 125
Jessie, 34
JETT: Francis, 47, 64
Jibson, 123
Jillian, 75
Jim, 7, 11, 14, 19, 21, 25, 34,
39, 40, 46, 51, 54, 60, 63, 67,
71, 72, 74, 77, 80, 85, 86, 87,
90, 96, 98, 99, 103, 106, 108,
110, 113, 114, 115, 120, 121,
125, 126
Jim Moore, 60, 61
Jim Winters, 101, 109
Jimes, 95
Jimmy, 101, 110
Jinny, 49, 63, 67, 78, 85, 94,
112
Jno, 106

73

Jo, 85, 108, 109
Joanna, 40, 65, 110
Job, 112
Joe, 10, 13, 17, 21, 24, 27, 31,
   34, 35, 38, 45, 47, 62, 64, 71,
   97, 98, 108, 110
Joe Lewis, 101
Joe Peyton, 101
Joe Simpson, 101, 109
Johanna, 115
John, 2, 3, 4, 5, 6, 7, 8, 9, 10,
   13, 15, 16, 17, 18, 20, 21, 22,
   23, 24, 25, 29, 30, 32, 33, 34,
   36, 39, 40, 45, 46, 47, 48, 50,
   52, 53, 54, 58, 60, 61, 62, 63,
   64, 65, 66, 67, 68, 69, 71, 73,
   74, 78, 80, 81, 83, 84, 85, 88,
   89, 90, 91, 93, 94, 95, 96, 97,
   98, 100, 101, 103, 104, 105,
   107, 109, 110, 111, 112, 113,
   114, 115, 118, 119, 120, 123,
   124, 125, 126
John Berry, 123
John Eldridge, 111
John Frank, 20
John Henry, 101, 102, 120
John Kent, 32
John L., 32
John Mann, 5
John Robert, 63, 72
John W., 32
John Wright, 34
Johnson, 104; Lucy, 91
JOHNSON: Joseph E., 3;
   Moses, 105; P.S., 80; Patty,
   91; Presley, 97; Samuel, 91;
   Sarah, 91
JOHNSTON: Richard H., 33
Jonah, 14, 57, 58, 66, 77
Jonas, 120, 126
Jonathan, 1, 17, 101
Jones, 68, 75
JONES: Ann A., 120;
   Cassander, 105; Charles,

120; Elizabeth, 21, 105;
   John, 17
Joseph, 3, 4, 7, 16, 20, 33, 49,
   53, 57, 58, 60, 63, 66, 68, 73,
   75, 79, 80, 85, 104, 109, 110,
   115, 119, 124, 126
Joseph Carter, 123
Joseph Henry, 80
Joseph Riley, 109
Josephine, 124
Joshing, 110
Joshua, 1, 5, 10, 14, 19, 21, 26,
   32, 34, 36, 40, 45, 57, 67, 68,
   94, 96, 97, 100, 101, 102,
   106, 109, 112, 113, 114, 125
Josiah, 3, 8, 80
Joy, 52, 116
Judah, 6, 36, 39, 40, 65, 104,
   118, 119, 123
Jude, 6, 14, 18, 40, 41, 68
Judith, 3, 8, 25, 41, 42, 51, 57,
   61, 98, 99, 117
Judy, 18, 20, 22, 24, 27, 29, 30,
   32, 34, 36, 39, 47, 49, 58, 59,
   64, 71, 79, 80, 88, 91, 95,
   110, 113, 115, 116, 120, 124
Jule, 6
Jules, 97
Julia, 5, 6, 18, 19, 54, 99, 101
Julia Ann, 61
Julia Francis, 23
Julian, 15, 58, 75, 79
Juliann, 111
Julianna, 76, 121
Julie, 46
Juliet, 4, 6, 15, 46, 60, 68, 72,
   73, 75, 100
June, 64, 97

Kate, 18, 119
Katy, 17, 96
KEEBLE: Anderson, 29; Fanny
   W, 40; Richard, 77
KEITH: Isham, 113; James, 21,
   106, 107; James A., 114;

Marshall, 106; Thomas, 114;
Thomas A, 106
Kelly, 114
KELLY: Alex D., 10; George
P., 10; James W., 10; John,
10; John P., 10; Margaret,
40; Richard P., 10; Sarah, 29
Kelsey, 69
Kemp, 62, 63, 99
KEMPER, 71; Charles, 94, 118;
John, 37; Susannah, 118
Keneford, 97
KENNARD: Molly, 77, 79;
Violet, 77, 120, 124
KENNEDY: Joseph H., 109
Kenneth, 87, 105, 106
KERCHEVAL: Elijah, 126;
Maria L, 126
KERFOOT: Daniel, 18; Daniel
S., 5
KERR: Dorcas, 61
KERTON: Frances, 117
KEYS: James A., 115; John A.,
112
KIETH: James, 112
Killy, 20
Kilzia, 114
KINCHELOE: Brandt, 57;
Elizabeth, 57; Hardwick, 57,
121; James, 57, 59, 76; Mary
Ann, 121, 126
King, 21
Kipey, 46
Kissiah, 123
Kitt, 47, 58, 64, 66, 73, 93, 119
Kitty, 4, 9, 11, 16, 18, 20, 22,
23, 26, 30, 31, 32, 34, 36, 41,
46, 51, 52, 54, 57, 58, 64, 65,
67, 71, 72, 75, 76, 78, 79, 80,
87, 90, 91, 95, 99, 101, 109,
110, 115, 118, 119
Kitty Cooper, 42
Kitty Riley, 109

LACEY: Mesha, 8; Meshech,
37
Lacy, 94
LAIOLER: Asa, 100
LAKE: Ann, 113, 120; James,
90, 93
LAMONT: Elizabeth, 9
Landon, 51
Landonia, 91, 123
LANE: Miss, 66
Larepta, 47
Lark, 40
Larkin, 110, 115, 121
LATHAM: Catherine W., 39;
Nancy, 13; Robert W., 99;
Thomas A, 99
LATHUM: Sarah, 51
Latto, 57
Laura, 6, 37, 42, 94, 100
Laurinda, 75
Laury, 24
Lavina, 41, 125
Lavinia, 58, 66, 96, 101, 123,
125
Lawrence, 5, 53, 71, 73, 78,
110, 115
LAWRENCE: Mason, 76
Lawson, 19, 96, 110, 112, 115,
125
Leah, 3, 80, 97, 102
Leak, 8
Leanne, 15
LEATH: Peggy, 9
Lee, 54, 80, 108, 113
LEE: Mary W., 29; Pamela, 109
Leias, 63
Leilia, 57
LEITCH: Philimon, 50
Lelah, 27, 73
Lemmon, 18, 123
Lemuel, 14, 89, 94
Lenna, 101
Lenney, 40
Lett, 76

Letty, 16, 32, 45, 65, 67, 68, 71, 73, 75, 78, 80, 94, 95, 96, 101, 103, 107
Leuanna, 121
Levi, 64, 95
Levina, 27, 41, 112
Levinia, 98, 100
Lewellen, 120
Lewis, 5, 9, 18, 22, 23, 24, 32, 34, 36, 37, 38, 39, 40, 41, 42, 45, 50, 53, 61, 64, 65, 67, 69, 73, 75, 82, 84, 95, 98, 99, 100, 102, 103, 104, 105, 106, 107, 109, 110, 114, 117, 120, 124, 125, 126
LEWIS: Anthony, 33; H.M., 113; Henry M., 33; James, 33; Kitty, 20; Lydia, 105, 107; Mary, 105; William, 20, 33, 34, 107
Lewis Bird, 75
Leytha, 50
Libby, 32
Liddy, 2, 36
Lige, 3
Lilly, 57, 119
Lin, 115
Lina, 47, 50, 86, 98
Linah, 80
Lindsey, 2, 65
Lindsey Moore, 60, 61
Linsey, 88, 100
Littleton, 67, 95, 122
Liza, 9, 30, 62
Lizetta, 73
Lizzy, 119
Logan, 47
LOMAX: John, 22, 32, 105; Miriam, 106; Susan, 106; Thomas, 105, 106
London, 1, 41
Lorends, 68
Lorenzo, 46, 57, 75
Lorinda, 41, 50, 52, 59
Lorry, 86

Lot, 35
Lotty, 112
Louema, 24
Louie, 4, 37
Louis, 13, 35
Louisa, 7, 17, 18, 21, 30, 34, 38, 40, 42, 43, 52, 57, 60, 62, 63, 73, 74, 80, 83, 84, 95, 96, 98, 110, 111, 114, 115, 121, 123
LOWERY: Ann, 51
LOWRY: Ann, 42, 43, 53
Luce, 19, 60
Lucelia, 87, 101, 105, 109, 117
Lucetta, 95
Lucinda, 5, 9, 15, 18, 21, 22, 23, 25, 32, 33, 34, 38, 46, 50, 58, 59, 64, 67, 71, 73, 78, 86, 89, 95, 98, 99, 100, 101, 102, 105, 106, 110, 115, 118, 125, 126
Lucinday, 13, 52
Lucious, 67
LUCUS: Fielding, 7
Lucy, 1, 2, 4, 5, 6, 9, 10, 11, 13, 14, 15, 16, 18, 19, 20, 21, 23, 24, 26, 27, 31, 32, 34, 35, 36, 37, 40, 51, 52, 57, 62, 63, 64, 65, 66, 68, 69, 72, 73, 75, 76, 78, 79, 80, 83, 84, 86, 87, 88, 90, 91, 93, 95, 96, 97, 98, 99, 100, 101, 104, 105, 106, 110, 111, 113, 114, 119, 121, 123, 125
Lucy Ann, 21, 66, 95, 101, 109
Lucy Ellen, 23
Lucy Feagan, 95
Lucy Gaines, 98
Lucy Helen, 95
Lucy Johnson, 91, 98
Lucy Malvin, 91
Ludley, 80
Ludwell, 18, 19, 51, 101, 118
Luellia, 16
Luther, 48

Lydda, 8
Lydia, 2, 6, 22, 33, 34, 40, 45,
    63, 77, 86, 93, 98, 100, 119,
    124

Macey, 104
Mack, 27
MACRAE: B.W., 46; James
    M., 18; John, 63; Sally Jane,
    46
Madaline, 110, 114
MADDAX: Hannah, 120;
    Thomas L., 77; William, 120
MADDUX: James D., 109;
    Thomas S., 81
Madison, 36, 57, 114
MADISON: Susan, 84
Madison Monimia, 80
Magdelana, 101
Mahala, 5, 7, 23, 36, 72, 75, 91,
    95, 99, 112
Mahalia, 23, 45
Major, 94, 109
Major Johnson, 101
Major Lewis, 57
Malinda, 19, 32, 39, 40, 64, 93,
    105, 110
MALLORY: Ann, 87
Malvin: Lucy, 91
Malvina, 22, 24, 33, 34, 40, 55,
    101
MANAFEE: Susan C, 95
Manah, 14
Manda, 68
Mandy, 110
Manimia, 110
Mann: Henry Lock, 5; Jack
    Thompson, 5; John, 5;
    Peggy, 5; Prudence, 5;
    Sylvia, 5; Thornton, 5;
    William, 5
Manscel, 66
Manuel, 10, 52, 58, 74, 101,
    103, 107, 115
Mapelia, 121

Marcia, 118
Marcus, 67
Margaret, 13, 14, 25, 39, 40, 41,
    48, 52, 57, 58, 61, 67, 68, 73,
    80, 83, 84, 85, 98, 99, 101,
    104, 105, 113, 118, 119, 125
Margaret Ann, 80
Marging, 32
Maria, 1, 2, 5, 6, 7, 10, 11, 13,
    15, 17, 18, 19, 21, 23, 24, 25,
    27, 31, 32, 34, 41, 45, 46, 47,
    48, 50, 52, 54, 55, 63, 64, 66,
    69, 71, 72, 73, 76, 77, 78, 80,
    81, 85, 88, 91, 94, 95, 96, 98,
    99, 102, 103, 104, 106, 107,
    109, 110, 112, 115, 118, 121,
    122, 124, 125, 126
Maria Louisa, 98
Mariah, 4, 7, 18, 22, 33, 37, 39,
    48, 52, 60, 65, 68, 69, 73, 84,
    85, 86, 88, 89, 100, 114, 115,
    119
Mariah Jr., 85
Marian, 60, 69
Marico, 115
Marie, 5
Marietta, 94
Marion, 65
Mark, 94, 96, 98, 99
Marriette, 107
Marsah, 95
Marshall, 6, 37, 67, 76, 95, 96,
    98, 99, 100, 110, 114
MARSHALL: Ann L, 79, 88;
    Ann L., 66, 73, 85; Ann S.,
    94; Fielding, 79; Fielding L.,
    66, 72, 85; James K., 55;
    John, 36; Margaret, 72;
    Margaret L., 67, 79, 85, 88,
    94; Mary, 72; Mrs., 59;
    Mumford, 94; Thomas, 58,
    66, 67, 72, 79, 85, 88, 94
Martha, 14, 24, 25, 27, 40, 46,
    48, 54, 60, 69, 74, 78, 80, 86,
    98, 99, 102, 103, 104, 105,

77

106, 110, 111, 114, 119, 120,
121, 123, 124, 126
Martha Ann, 57, 96
Martin, 3, 4, 5, 6, 10, 13, 21,
23, 39, 49, 64, 77, 81, 99,
104, 108, 112, 117
MARTIN: Ann C., 27; Elias,
27, 30; Elizabeth M., 114;
Francis, 79; George W, 27;
George W., 30, 62; John, 27;
Lucy, 79; Mary, 62; Polly,
27; William E., 27, 62
Mary, 2, 3, 4, 5, 6, 7, 8, 9, 10,
13, 14, 15, 16, 17, 18, 19, 20,
21, 22, 23, 24, 25, 27, 30, 31,
32, 33, 34, 35, 36, 37, 38, 39,
40, 41, 42, 43, 45, 46, 47, 49,
51, 53, 54, 57, 58, 60, 61, 62,
63, 64, 65, 66, 67, 68, 69, 71,
72, 73, 75, 76, 80, 84, 89, 90,
93, 94, 95, 96, 98, 99, 100,
101, 103, 105, 106, 107, 108,
109, 110, 112, 114, 116, 117,
118, 119, 120, 121, 123, 124,
125, 126
Mary Ann, 17, 21, 41, 50, 52,
68, 75, 80, 93, 96, 103, 111,
123, 124, 126
Mary Ellen, 101, 113, 123
Mary Frances, 52, 101
Mary Glascock, 42
Mary Jane, 42, 43, 62, 68, 97
Mary Steptoe, 32
Maryann, 45, 121
Maryanne, 123
Mason, 22, 33, 46, 47, 54, 71,
96
MASSEY: Ned, 93
MASSIE: Ann, 123; Emily,
120; J.W., 34; John, 123;
John M, 120; John W., 34;
Nancy, 11, 24; Thomas BR,
100; William, 24
Mat, 110
Mathew, 86

Mathilda, 52
Matilda, 4, 7, 8, 14, 15, 19, 22,
23, 26, 32, 34, 38, 46, 52, 58,
60, 61, 63, 64, 71, 73, 74, 75,
78, 80, 81, 90, 94, 95, 96, 98,
100, 101, 103, 104, 107, 109,
110, 111, 113, 115, 123, 125
Matilda Caroline, 71
Matildy, 15
Matthew, 77, 79, 83, 86, 90
MATTHEWS: Squire E., 68
MAXWELL: Thomas, 121
May, 38, 116
Mayullia, 120
McAllister, 83, 86, 87
McCLENAHAM: Mrs., 34
McCORMICK: Charles N., 79;
Hugh, 48; Mary A., 79
McCOY: Walter, 94, 122;
William, 109
McDANIEL: Henry I, 118
McDONALD: Ebbin, 27
McGEORGE: John, 9
McMULLEN: Margaret B., 104
Melford, 32, 87, 122
Melinda, 15, 18, 20, 25, 27, 31,
52, 65, 72, 73, 74, 98, 108,
112, 117, 121
Melissa, 112
Melville, 118
Melvina, 49, 59
MENIFEE: Henry, 68
Menty, 91
Mesciny, 63
Meshach, 67, 122
Michael, 94
MICHAEL: Mary, 5
Mildred, 29, 35, 40, 74, 86, 98,
102, 103, 106, 111, 115
Miles, 6
Milford, 105, 106, 107, 115
Milford Jr, 107
Milly, 1, 5, 6, 10, 17, 18, 23,
24, 25, 27, 31, 36, 37, 38, 39,
41, 49, 51, 54, 55, 57, 58, 60,

62, 67, 71, 72, 73, 78, 82, 90, 95, 97, 98, 100, 101, 103, 104, 106, 107, 110, 113, 114, 118, 122, 123, 125
Milly Allen, 101
Milton, 8, 17, 25, 39, 57, 60
MILTON: James F, 121
Mima, 6, 35, 39, 46, 50, 53, 97, 102, 122
Mima Maria, 112
Mimah, 34
Mimes, 59
Mimia, 6
Mimy, 84
Mina, 74, 99
Minam, 109
Miner, 4, 60, 61
Minerva, 76, 106
Minny, 6, 60, 94
Minta, 64
MINTER: Malinda, 89; Sinai, 72; Sinar, 52; Susan, 52
Minty, 25, 47
Mira, 107
Mirah, 52, 53
Miriah, 61, 74, 78, 83
Missy, 84, 106
MITCHELL: Judith, 54
MOFFIT: Mrs, 122
Molly, 15, 46, 54, 57, 71, 73, 75, 78, 79, 80, 99, 100, 104, 107, 113, 120, 121, 123
Monimia, 98
Monroe, 69
MONROE: John, 5
MONRONEY: William, 53
MONSHEAD: Charles, 67
MONTGOMERY: William, 22, 33
Moona, 20, 25
MOONE: Jesse R., 90
MOONEY, 97; Emily, 57; Jesse, 17; Jesse R., 97; Nicholas, 17, 34; Samuel, 17; William, 17

Moora, 11
Moore: Jim, 61; Lindsey, 61
MOORHEAD: Charles, 67; Lewis, 25, 39, 57
Morcah, 97
Mordeca, 86
MOREHEAD: James, 124; Louis, 8; Presley, 109; Presley W., 38
Morgan, 63
MORGAN: Capt. Joseph, 114; Caroline, 16; J, 124; James, 16; Joseph, 96; Mary, 16; William, 16, 47
Morganna, 101
Morris, 10
MORRIS: A., 21; Alexander, 21; Richard A., 21; Richard P., 1, 2; Sander, 21
Mortimer, 60, 68
Morton, 6, 18, 19, 20, 24, 25, 53, 83, 94, 118
Mose, 111
Moses, 6, 9, 14, 15, 24, 25, 29, 33, 35, 36, 40, 41, 46, 50, 52, 54, 60, 63, 65, 72, 76, 94, 95, 96, 97, 98, 99, 101, 108, 109, 117, 118, 119, 121, 124
Moses Smith, 109
Moses Winters, 101
MOTT: Ann, 40; Louisa, 40; William, 40, 52
MURPHY: John, 68
MURRAY: Alfred, 18, 111; Catherine, 18, 19; James, 18; James E., 111; Nancy, 97, 122; Reuben, 111, 117; Reuben J., 111; Samuel, 85
MURREY: Josiah, 65
MURRY: Josiah, 113; Nancy, 102
Nace, 4, 6, 24, 32, 34, 35, 48, 65, 77, 105, 106, 118
Nancy, 2, 3, 4, 5, 7, 8, 9, 10, 11, 14, 15, 16, 17, 19, 20, 21, 22,

23, 25, 31, 32, 34, 36, 38, 40,
41, 46, 48, 50, 52, 54, 57, 58,
64, 65, 68, 71, 73, 74, 75, 78,
80, 83, 84, 90, 93, 94, 96, 98,
100, 101, 103, 104, 106, 107,
110, 113, 114, 121, 124, 125
Nancy Carter, 71, 78
Nancy Jane, 74
Nanny, 66
Nat, 74, 96, 99, 104, 110, 114
Nathan, 3, 9, 118
Nathaniel, 17, 76
Natus, 50, 76, 84, 86, 99, 106
Neal, 94
NEAL: John, 79
Neale, 89
Ned, 5, 6, 14, 15, 17, 19, 22, 32,
38, 45, 48, 51, 54, 55, 63, 78,
82, 85, 91, 93, 100, 105, 110,
112, 113, 115, 117, 120, 123
Ned Brooks, 46
Nelly, 3, 4, 6, 9, 10, 17, 21, 29,
37, 39, 40, 45, 49, 54, 57, 63,
67, 68, 71, 78, 80, 92, 112
Nelson, 7, 23, 36, 38, 40, 41,
53, 54, 55, 67, 68, 85, 110,
115, 123
NELSON: Eleanor, 38, 69;
George, 60; James M., 113;
Joseph, 66, 76; Thomas, 122
Nicholas, 8, 71
Nick, 22, 33, 36, 41, 55
Nimrod, 7, 8, 42, 57, 59, 62, 95,
115, 119, 120
Nina, 83
Noah, 73
NOLAND: Burr Powell, 15;
Catherine Mary, 15; Richard
W., 15; Thomas Lloyd, 15
Nora, 6
Norris, 97
NORRIS: Ann, 76; Joseph, 73,
76, 93; Thaddius, 76
Norsisa, 92
NORWILL: P., 63; Peyton, 63

Nuly Van, 101
Nussi, 115
NUTT: Mr, 105

O'BANNON: Armistead, 42;
Fanny, 49; Frances, 80, 88,
112; James, 49; Jane L., 49;
Jesse, 103, 105; Joseph, 22;
Presley N., 53; Thomas, 39,
49, 65; William, 49
O'REAR: Benjamin H., 106
Oatway, 79
Obid, 60, 86
Oby, 58, 67
Octavia, 60
OGILVIE: John, 6, 97, 106
Oliver, 62
OLIVER: John, 85; Mary, 67;
Sibby, 85
Olleway, 104
Opam, 7
Orange, 22, 123
Orich, 115
Orlando, 58
Orra, 87, 105, 106
Osborn, 18, 36, 51, 52
Oscar, 21, 41, 42, 45, 52, 86,
125
Osten, 3, 9
OWENS: Cuthbert, 69;
Cuthburt, 96

PADGETT: Dempsey, 109
Page, 8, 16, 65, 74, 77
PAGE: Cam, 119; Corban B.,
116; Corbin B, 118
Page Sand, 101
Paiss, 1
PALMER: Mary, 37
Pam, 53
Pamela, 98, 99
Parker, 32, 34
PARKER: Betty, 68; Jno, 25;
Mrs., 48

80

PARR: Caroline Mary, 74;
Hannah, 21; Henry W., 74;
James McDonald, 74;
Joseph, 21; William, 21, 74
Patiena, 110
Patience, 4, 5, 16, 48, 98, 99,
114, 119
Patrick, 23
Patrick Ellis, 101
Patsy, 4, 13, 27, 32, 34, 41, 42,
60, 61, 89, 101, 122
Patty, 5, 11, 13, 14, 15, 27, 30,
61, 63, 64, 67, 76, 82, 91, 93,
113, 116, 120
Paul, 15, 19, 96, 112, 125
PAYNE: Amos, 71; Arthur M.,
65, 109; Catharine, 59;
Daniel, 24, 66, 83; Daniel S.,
22; Doc., 87; Elizabeth, 24,
105; Eloisa G., 39; Enus,
106; Fanny P., 21; Frances
M., 104; Frances Rowena,
104; George, 20; Holander,
20; Jesse, 88; Jessy, 90;
John, 17, 24, 66; Judith S.,
112; Mary Annie, 104;
Robert A., 111; Sally, 83,
112; Thomas, 20; Virginia,
65; William, 65
Payton, 125
PAYTON: Eliza G., 24;
Margaret C., 24
PECK: Susan, 9; William, 9
Peggy, 6, 7, 15, 19, 22, 31, 34,
36, 45, 51, 52, 53, 61, 63, 64,
68, 69, 76, 79, 84, 96, 101,
104, 110, 113, 114, 115, 125
Peggy Locust, 109
Peggy Mann, 5
Pembroke, 109
Pembroke Pollard, 101
Pemmy, 123
Pender, 32
Penny, 57

PENQUITE: Joseph, 77; Kezia,
75; Keziah, 77; William, 75,
77, 85
Pensey, 59
Perry, 68
Peter, 2, 3, 5, 8, 9, 11, 14, 17,
18, 20, 23, 25, 26, 30, 31, 32,
34, 35, 36, 37, 38, 40, 42, 46,
48, 49, 51, 52, 59, 61, 63, 64,
66, 67, 73, 75, 78, 80, 83, 86,
88, 91, 95, 100, 104, 105,
107, 110, 113, 114, 115, 117,
122, 123, 125
PETERS: Ann, 64; Elizabeth,
13, 81; James, 91, 121;
Mary, 23
PETTIT: Catey, 14; Catherine
Y, 19; John H., 14, 18
Peyton, 23, 98
PEYTON: Chandler, 24;
Elizabeth, 24; John Scott,
24; R C, 121; Richard H.,
24, 83; Robert, 24
Phanley, 115
Phebe, 1, 8, 10, 33, 45, 62, 63,
76, 85
Phelix, 60
Phidelia, 34
Phil, 42, 51, 54, 57, 59, 60, 73,
75, 78, 83, 87, 88, 90, 100,
101, 103, 105, 106, 109, 110,
113, 117
Philip, 20, 24, 32, 34, 50, 73,
78, 80, 86, 95, 119, 125
Philip Compton, 123
Phillip, 66, 71, 96, 123
PHILLIPS: John P., 45
Phillis, 14, 24, 41, 52, 58, 64,
66, 71, 72, 103, 110, 114,
126
Phily, 99
Phoebe, 71, 96, 114
PICKETT: Lavinea F., 45
PIERCE: Peter, 33
PILCHER: A.S., 113

Pleasant, 45, 58, 66, 101
Pocha, 110
Pollard, 14
POLLARD: Abner, 92;
    Catharine Y, 117; Catherine,
    108; Elizabeth, 108, 115;
    Elizabeth J, 117; Isaac J,
    117; John P., 92; Katharine,
    115; Margaret, 108, 115,
    117; Mary, 95, 108, 118;
    Mary H, 117; Mildred, 108,
    115, 117; Mildred A., 108;
    P. H., 118; Patrick H, 117;
    Patrick H., 95
Polly, 5, 9, 10, 15, 21, 30, 34,
    36, 57, 58, 61, 67, 71, 72, 73,
    76, 80, 88, 94, 97, 98, 99,
    101, 104, 121, 123
Polly Ann, 115
Polly Green, 99
Polly Hurly, 101
Polly Precious, 101
Pomp, 13, 67
Pompey, 5, 68, 83, 86
Pomsy, 71
Pope, 95
POPE: Sara, 37
PORTER: Alex, 109; John, 74;
    Samuel, 107
Presley, 79
Price, 17, 95
Pride, 74
PRIEST: Henry, 72; Mason,
    117; Sarah, 24; Sarah H., 66;
    Tellous, 117; Thomas, 58,
    68, 75; William, 24; Willis,
    117
Prince, 105
Prior, 15
Priscilla, 22, 32, 33, 34, 46, 50,
    81
Priss, 60
Prissy Jane, 101
Prudence, 24, 25
Prudence Mann, 5

Psalter, 75
Pulchera, 106
Pulchin, 105
Pulchisia, 87
PULLEN: Samuel, 107
PULLER: Sarah, 104
Puss, 79

Rachel, 1, 2, 3, 5, 7, 8, 10, 15,
    17, 19, 21, 25, 31, 38, 51, 52,
    62, 63, 66, 67, 68, 75, 80, 83,
    86, 87, 89, 96, 102, 106, 124,
    125
Rachel Jr., 5
RAGE: Corban B., 54
RAGER, 60
Raleigh, 109, 114
Ralph, 3, 9, 54, 57, 102, 123
Randall, 46, 57, 75, 78, 80, 99,
    107, 113, 121
RANDALL: Agness, 16;
    William O., 16
Randel, 73, 90
Randolph, 71, 76
RANDOLPH: Elizabeth H., 40
RANSDELL: Horace, 109
READ: Maria Louisa, 103
Rebecca, 5, 18, 48, 72
Rebecca Jane, 109
RECTER: Elias H., 109
RECTOR: Benjamin, 9;
    Elizabeth, 25; Franklin, 120;
    Henry, 3, 9; Jane, 123; John,
    9; Susannah, 68; Thomas A,
    78, 125; Willis, 9
Redmond, 71
REID: Alexander, 33
Reuben, 5, 6, 9, 15, 17, 19, 39,
    45, 48, 49, 50, 58, 59, 62, 64,
    66, 71, 73, 78, 80, 91, 98, 99,
    100, 107, 110, 112, 115, 124,
    125
Reuben Jr, 114
Richard, 3, 4, 6, 8, 10, 13, 18,
    19, 20, 24, 40, 42, 48, 53, 57,

60, 68, 73, 80, 83, 98, 113, 119
RICHARD: Felix, 109; Octavia, 65
Richard Henry, 98, 101, 106
Richards, 21
Riley, 6, 41, 42, 53
RILEY: John, 115; Lewis, 115
Risper, 114
RIVES: Jonathan, 42
RIXEY: Richard, 97; Samuel, 57
ROACH: Elizabeth, 17
Rob, 99
Robbin, 6, 19, 71, 72, 73
ROBERSON: Agnes, 113; W., 35; William, 68
Robert, 5, 7, 9, 10, 15, 30, 31, 32, 34, 36, 45, 48, 50, 54, 57, 58, 62, 63, 67, 71, 76, 80, 84, 90, 93, 95, 96, 98, 99, 104, 109, 112, 115, 117, 124, 125, 126
Robert Anthony, 35
Robert Green, 124
Robert Nelson, 35
Robert Pollard, 101, 109
Robert Sr., 20
Robert Williams, 101, 109
Robert, Jr., 20
Robertson, 24
Robin, 8, 34, 46, 49, 58, 59, 66, 69
Robinson, 77, 83, 118
ROBINSON: Lydia, 1
Robison, 118
ROBISON: Agnes, 120
Roderick, 78
Roger, 36, 41, 73
ROGERS: Joanna, 15; Mary, 21; Robert, 15
Rolly, 54, 119
Rosanna, 41, 57
Rose, 6, 7, 15, 19, 20, 21, 22, 23, 25, 32, 34, 36, 47, 51, 52,

53, 54, 63, 64, 96, 98, 102, 104, 105, 113, 117, 119, 124, 125, 126
ROSE: E.F., 109; Mary L.H., 45; Robert, 45; Robert H., 45, 100; William, 45
Rose Ann, 110, 114
Rosetta, 54, 83, 84, 86, 99
Ross, 105
ROSSER: F. T., 118; Priscilla, 41
Rosy, 86
ROUTT: Peter, 73
Rover, 119
ROWLES: Elisah, 111; Elisha, 111, 123; Nancy Emiley, 111; Robert, 111, 123; Samuel, 111, 123; William, 111, 123
Roy, 32
ROY: Lydia, 67
Rozella, 104
Rozetty, 117
Rush, 6
Russell, 7, 52
RUSSELL: James, 109
RUST: Benjamin, 35, 51, 60; Bushrod, 5, 18; Elizabeth, 32, 51; James, 35, 51; James L., 35; John, 51; John L, 52; John L., 60
Ruth, 15, 19, 23, 50, 59, 64, 124
Ruthy, 101
RYLAND: Alfred, 71

S. Patterson, 64
Sabley, 94
Sabra, 17, 20, 24
Sabrey, 112
SAKE: James, 98
Sal, 6
Sally, 4, 9, 13, 14, 18, 22, 23, 24, 25, 27, 30, 32, 33, 34, 35, 36, 45, 50, 57, 58, 59, 62, 63, 64, 67, 71, 73, 78, 80, 83, 85,

48; Martha, 24; Mary, 24;
Sally, 24; Sarah, 23
Shadrach, 37, 98, 114, 117, 122
Shadrack, 52, 67, 68, 72, 75,
99, 100, 110
Shakespear, 98
SHALKETT: John, 24; Lewis,
24
Shapley, 2
Sharlotte, 15, 16, 18, 25, 37, 60,
61, 79, 85
SHARPE: Arthur, 23; Frances,
23; Sinfield, 23
SHELKET: John, 2; Nancy, 2
SHIELDS: William, 49
Shinner, 33
SHINNEZ: U., 35
Shirley, 61
SHUMATE: Elizabeth, 98;
Fanny Pitts, 39; Jno, 106;
John Taliaferro, 39;
Taliaferro, 39, 41
Sias, 73
Sidna, 13, 81
Sidney, 6, 7, 8, 15, 18, 54, 61,
63, 75, 86
Silas, 10, 34, 88, 91, 103, 120,
121
Silla, 24
Sillar, 2, 8, 39, 51, 71, 106, 115
Silva, 95, 107
Silvy, 8, 23, 47, 80, 110
Simas, 99
Simon, 5, 14, 15, 18, 19, 36, 40,
47, 51, 52, 54, 57, 64, 66, 72,
75, 86, 98, 112, 113, 118
Simon Jackson, 101
SIMPLETON: R., 1
Sina, 116
Sinah, 3, 8, 82, 91, 101, 113
Sinai, 120
SINCLAIR: French, 98; James
A., 98; Nelly, 84
Siner, 19, 30

SINGLETON: Lucinda, 54;
Robert, 5, 18
Sinna, 111
SISSON: Mary, 89
Sissy Ann, 101
Sittemer, 24
SKINKER: Harriet, 114; James,
108; John, 108; Mary I., 115;
Mary J., 108; Thomas, 115;
Tom, 108; William, 108,
110, 114
Slace, 93
SMALL: George, 117
SMALLWOOD: Alice, 114;
George, 114
Smith, 68, 75, 110, 114
SMITH: Alex, 86; Ann, 32;
Augustine, 20; Buckner A.,
72; C.B., 60; Capt. Jno. P.,
83; Charles B., 59, 82, 86,
113; Edward, 7, 22; Eleanor,
87, 102, 115; Elizabeth, 41,
42; Enoch, 2, 51; Frances,
114; George, 114; George
W.F., 97, 109; Hedgman, 33;
Hugh G., 87; Jackalina, 87;
James, 50, 87, 102; James P.,
50; James W., 71; Johann,
24; John, 71, 113; John P.,
86, 104; Joseph, 22, 59, 113;
Joseph A., 50; Leonidas,
114; Margaret, 11, 24, 119;
Maria C., 87; Marshall, 7;
Martha B., 50; Mary G, 103;
Miss, 59, 60; Mrs., 87;
Patrick, 114; Polly, 88;
Presley, 114; Sarah, 71;
Thomas, 63; Thomas M., 50,
59; Thomas W, 51; Walter
A, 119; Walter A., 114;
Walter C., 50; William, 60,
64, 114; William V., 87
SMITH Jr.: Augustine, 14
SMOOT: John, 90; Margaret,
94, 103, 111, 113, 124

Snaitolle, 110
Solo, 62, 63
Solomon, 40, 54, 58, 66, 85,
    110, 114
Sophia, 6, 17, 24, 25, 36, 38,
    41, 47, 64, 83, 95, 98, 106
Sophy, 7, 98
SOUGHBOROUGH: Mrs., 63
Sowers, 118
SOWERS: Daniel, 91
Spencer, 4, 13, 15, 16, 18, 35,
    36, 38, 47, 52, 53, 54, 57, 71,
    73, 78, 91, 97, 99, 103, 107,
    119
Spencer Westley, 57
SPILMAN: George, 93
SPURLOCK: Isaiah, 113
Squire, 51
Stafford, 22
Stanton, 2, 110, 115
STARKE: James, 2, 5, 25;
    Rooham, 2
Staunton, 10
STEFHENE: Thomas, 2
Stephen, 6, 8, 53, 58, 67, 71,
    72, 73, 78, 90, 93, 98, 103,
    110, 114
STEPHENS: William, 41, 49,
    74, 97, 123
Sterling, 64, 66, 72
STEVEN: Charles J., 109
STEWART: Allen, 9; William,
    46, 69, 75
STINSON: Benjamin, 115;
    James, 30, 115; William, 115
STONE: Eliza Ann, 95; Jno,
    74; John, 109; Mary, 17, 60;
    Mrs., 61; Richard, 109;
    William, 17, 39
STONE, Jr.: William, 60
Strickling, 58
STRIGHT: William, 49
STRINGFELLOW: James, 23
Strother, 17, 18, 25, 64, 87, 97,
    102, 110, 114, 119, 122, 125

STROTHER: Alexander, 65;
    Elizabeth, 89; Enoch, 65,
    111; Hedgeman, 65; Jackson
    Farrow, 89; James, 5, 19;
    Jeremiah, 40, 65; Jno, 63;
    John, 40, 61, 64, 113; Juliett
    Ann, 89; Lewis, 89, 91, 126;
    Lucy Cornelia, 89; Mary,
    124; Nancy, 89; Reuben, 61,
    63, 76; Sarah Ann, 65;
    Susannah, 65
Suckey, 49, 54, 112
Sucky, 19, 21, 48, 57, 63, 71
SUDDOTH: John, 71; Mrs., 71;
    Susan A, 122
Sukey, 14, 18, 22, 23, 42, 46,
    99, 109
SULLIVAN: James B, 125; JC,
    125; John C., 125; John C.,
    23, 35, 37, 66, 89; L.O., 80;
    Luther O., 109; Mary, 80;
    Mrs, 61; Mrs., 61; Warner,
    67, 125; Willis, 35
SUMMER: Edward, 47; Jane
    E., 67
Summerfield, 74, 103
SUMMERS: E., 35; Edward,
    67, 90, 123; George
    Wellington, 121; GeorgeW,
    123; Jane E., 90; John E,
    123; Sally E, 121; Sarah,
    123; Sarah Virginia, 121;
    William L, 123
SUNCEFORD: Mary, 99
Susan, 5, 6, 10, 13, 15, 23, 24,
    25, 32, 34, 36, 41, 42, 46, 57,
    62, 63, 64, 65, 73, 75, 76, 78,
    80, 86, 87, 91, 96, 97, 98,
    101, 102, 104, 106, 107, 110,
    112, 114, 115, 125
Susan Ann, 101, 109
Susan Beakeley, 109
Susan Smith, 109
Susan Tenles, 101
Susannah, 10, 13, 80

Tom, 2, 3, 4, 6, 9, 10, 14, 15,
  18, 19, 22, 24, 29, 30, 31, 32,
  33, 34, 40, 45, 46, 48, 54, 57,
  58, 62, 63, 65, 68, 73, 74, 75,
  91, 93, 95, 96, 98, 99, 102,
  104, 107, 110, 113, 114, 115,
  121, 123, 124, 126
Tom Ash, 58, 66
Tom Jefferson, 66
Tom Turner, 123
TOMKINS: Rob R., 109
TOMLIN: John, 26, 47, 48;
  William, 66, 79
Tomsey, 46
TONGUE: Ann L., 54; John W,
  77; Johnze, 54, 69; Robert,
  54
Tony, 17, 24, 75
Townsend, 40, 99
Townshend, 102
Townson, 68
TRACEY: James, 77; Lewis, 91
Travis, 73, 76, 94, 100
TREPLET: Pamela, 104
Trilus, 78, 85
TRIPLETT: Nancy, 74
Tristran, 125
Troy, 7
Trular, 114
Tulip, 6, 52, 60, 84, 123
TULLOSS: John, 41; Rodham,
  41, 93, 106
Tully, 117
Turner, 7, 51, 52, 64
TURNER: Jackson, 83; John, 6;
  Louisa, 121; Thomas, 74;
  Thomas B, 124
Tye, 15
TYLER: Nathaniel, 54, 75, 84
Tylor, 22

Uriah, 67, 68
UTTERBACK: Armistead, 3,
  6; Elijah, 3; French, 3;
  Harmon, 1, 3, 4, 17; Harriet

N., 4; James, 3; Lucy, 4;
  Margaret, 4; Maria Louisa,
  4, 87, 99; Mary, 4, 47;
  Nathaniel, 1, 3, 29, 89;
  Thompson, 3; Thornton, 1,
  6; Wilfred, 103; Willis, 3, 4,
  5, 21

Vall, 119
Velvet, 60
Venice, 6
Venor, 45
Venus, 15, 17, 19, 35, 45, 55,
  58, 59, 66, 96, 112
Viann, 38
Vick, 53
Vicky, 58, 66
Victoria, 110, 115
Vienna, 40, 99
Vince, 119
Vincent, 15, 32, 34, 64, 74, 99
Vine, 24
Vinny, 85, 86, 119
Violet, 6, 7, 15, 19, 20, 38, 39,
  40, 41, 45, 58, 66, 74, 86, 93,
  96, 112, 113, 121, 124, 125
Violet Jr, 125
Virgen, 98
Virginia, 64, 79, 80, 101, 107,
  109, 120
Visa, 14, 24
VOWLES: Newton, 109

WALDEN: Col., 87
Walker, 73, 74, 101, 103, 110,
  114
WALKER: Edward, 24;
  Frances, 24; Hephzabah,
  118; James W., 74; John, 14;
  John W., 108; Margaret, 23
Wallace, 76, 96, 99
WALLACE: Elizabeth E, 124;
  James W.M., 35; Mary E,
  124; Mary E., 57; William
  W., 57

Walter Withers, 7
Wansee, 37
WARD: B, 113; B., 91;
Benkeley, 98
WARDEN: Thom B., 65
WARDER: Elizabeth, 98
Warner, 46, 57, 75, 81, 100,
102; Elizabeth, 68; Fanny,
68; George, 68; Henry, 68;
James, 68; Lewis, 68;
Parker, 68
Warren, 87, 101, 105, 106
Wash, 36, 96
Washington, 3, 4, 8, 17, 24, 32,
34, 50, 57, 71, 73, 77, 78, 96,
97, 99, 100, 101, 104, 107,
109, 110, 114, 115, 125
WASHINGTON: John M., 63;
Temple M., 100
Washington Smith, 101
Water, 37
Watson, 57
WATSON: M.P., 80
Watt, 16, 51, 52
WEATHERBY: Jane, 6
Weaver, 15
WEAVER: Christiana, 65;
Christiana E., 66, 98; Jacob,
14, 26, 98; James, 65; James
M., 94, 95; John, 99; Joseph,
98; Mary, 14, 26; Richard
A., 66, 98; Samuel, 16, 51,
65, 98; Telman, 98; William,
65, 99; William T., 98
Webster, 92
Weeden, 110, 124
WEEDEN: Nimrod, 31
Weedon, 89, 114
WEEDON: William, 2
WEEKS: James, 60
WELCH: Alexander, 38, 39;
Benjamin, 40; Catharine, 40;
Edward, 40; Frances A., 81;
James, 62; John, 40; John N.,
81; Kitty, 33; Luther, 80;

Sylvester, 33, 39, 40, 42;
William M., 40
WELCH Sr.: Sylvester, 38
Welford, 65
Wellington, 76, 83, 86, 87, 99
Wendley, 14
Wensor, 124
Wesley, 7, 15, 17, 19, 29, 45,
50, 80, 84, 86, 93, 99, 106,
112, 123
WEST: B., 23; Benjamin, 23;
Nicholas L., 23; Silas M.,
53, 66
Westley, 23, 57, 60, 91
Westward, 6
WHARTON: Isaac, 119
WHEATBY: Lucretia, 22
White, 98, 99
WHITE: John, 88, 100
Whiting, 45
WHITING: Thomas, 13
Whiting Sr., 45
WHITLEY: Susan, 116, 119
WHORTON: Harriet, 78
WICKLIFFE: Andrew Jackson,
79; David, 79, 80, 88, 89;
Elizabeth Ann, 79; Leonard
Kenrick, 79; Margaretta
Susan, 79; Mildred Sarah,
79; Robert Horace, 79
Wiles, 118
Wiley, 46, 54
Wilford, 6
Wilfred, 93
Will, 30, 36, 58, 66, 67, 72, 122
William, 2, 5, 7, 8, 9, 10, 11,
13, 14, 15, 16, 17, 18, 19, 20,
21, 23, 24, 26, 29, 30, 31, 32,
34, 35, 37, 40, 41, 42, 48, 51,
52, 53, 58, 59, 60, 62, 63, 64,
65, 66, 69, 72, 74, 77, 79, 80,
83, 84, 85, 86, 87, 90, 91, 93,
94, 95, 96, 97, 98, 99, 100,
101, 103, 104, 105, 106, 108,
109, 110, 113, 114, 115, 119,

120, 121, 122, 123, 124, 125, 126
WILLIAM: Mary H., 98
William Bradford, 101
William Carter, 101
William Champ, 117
William Elgin, 4
William Ellis, 101
William Henry, 101
William Hunter, 109
William Jackson, 122
William Jones, 4
William Mann, 5
William Miller, 32
William Morton, 11
William Riley, 101, 109
William Simpson, 101, 109
William Stewart, 2
William Sydnor, 16
William Thibb, 101
Williams, 24
WILLIAMS: Jemima, 123; Lewis, 22; Mary H., 13
Willis, 8, 10, 15, 18, 19, 20, 22, 23, 25, 31, 33, 42, 46, 62, 63, 75, 79, 80, 95, 99, 102, 104, 109, 110, 111, 113, 114, 117, 124
WILLIS: Maria, 55
Willis Pollard, 101
Willoby, 36
Willoughby, 38, 75, 98
Willy, 20
Wilson, 18, 66, 94, 95, 97, 118
WILSON: Harriet, 81
Windson, 52
Windsor, 14
Windsor Jr., 25
Windsor Sr., 25
WINE: Fielding, 16
WINN: Jasmine, 58

Winny, 2, 3, 4, 5, 15, 18, 29, 32, 36, 38, 40, 47, 51, 54, 58, 59, 60, 63, 66, 67, 69, 72, 73, 75, 76, 79, 80, 81, 85, 86, 87, 88, 90, 91, 97, 98, 99, 104, 106, 107, 110, 111, 112, 115
Winslow, 34
Winston, 83, 117
WINTER: Melinda, 122
Withers: Becky, 91; Sam, 91; Thornton, 91
WITHERS: Catherine, 74; Daniel, 52, 68; Elizabeth C., 3; H.C., 90; Henry, 72; Horace C., 91, 115; Horatio C., 87; James, 7, 9, 41, 52, 112; Jesse H., 109; Louisa, 3; Margaret M., 74; Martin, 52; P. H., 119; Pickett, 52; Samuel, 20, 52; Thomas J., 98; Walter, 7
WOLDEN: S, 124
WOODSIDE: Clary, 8; Elizabeth, 8; Mary, 8; Sally, 8; William, 8; William A., 8
WOOLF: Ann C, 126
WRIGHT: Robert L, 121; William, 98
WYCKOFF: Elizabeth, 20, 21; Hannah, 121; William, 124

Yancy, 83
Yarrow, 78, 85
YEATMAN: George E., 54; Walter M., 11, 26; William T., 11
Yuly, 3

Zachary, 2
Zilla, 98
Zilpha, 46

VOLUME III

WILL BOOKS 21 – 31

1847 – 1869

, Betty Johnson, 92
, Ida Belle Lightfoot, 92
, Marj__i_, 41
_isiah, 51
Aaron, 2, 31, 41, 42, 48, 83, 92, 95, 97, 99, 102, 104, 109
Aaron Bennley, 44
Aaron Roberts, 48
Aaron Washington, 92
Abba, 50, 90
Abigail, 22
Abner, 38, 39, 49, 51
Abner Moro, 10
Abraham, 6, 20, 37, 46, 62, 68, 71
Abram, 6, 18, 22, 104, 105, 114
Absalom, 58, 59, 60, 69, 107, 108
Ada, 51, 55, 75, 87, 88, 93, 101, 108, 120
ADAIR: Jane, 106
Adaline, 15, 17, 20, 29, 35, 43, 74, 91, 96, 101, 108
Adam, 20, 77, 84, 99, 100, 105, 107, 118
ADAMS: Albert G., 57; Elizabeth M., 15; Ella, 81; Felicia C., 57; Frances, 15; George, 15; Harriet, 116; Harriet W., 15; Helen M., 57; James, 62; Margaret W., 57; Mary, 15; Matilda R., 102; Mrs., 117; Robert L., 69; Samuel W., 21; Sarah C., 57; Sydnor B., 15; Thomas, 15; Thomas A., 69, 70; Thomas J., 105; Thomas T.,

80, 91, 96; Thomas Turner, 111; Willis, 15, 57
Addison, 51, 75, 90, 93, 101, 108, 114, 120
Adelaide, 21, 29, 52, 55, 103
Adelia, 56
Adeline, 26, 45, 53, 67, 83, 114, 118
Adolphus, 37, 53, 70
Aggy, 25, 35, 65, 81, 84, 93, 100, 101, 120, 121
Agnes, 10, 22, 80, 95, 103, 112
Ailsey, 57, 84
Alamedia, 77
Alban, 53
Albert, 2, 3, 4, 10, 15, 16, 18, 20, 22, 25, 28, 34, 36, 37, 39, 45, 52, 54, 56, 57, 58, 59, 60, 62, 66, 68, 69, 70, 71, 77, 79, 80, 95, 97, 101, 104
Albert Chapman, 92
Albert Jackson, 92
Alberta, 50
Alcinda, 3, 40, 56, 105, 106
Aldridge, 2, 18, 20, 39, 57, 81, 105, 117
Alec, 3, 109
Aleck, 48, 66, 69
Alevia, 53
Alex, 12, 105
Alex Talbert, 48
Alexander, 2, 7, 22, 33, 34, 39, 40, 49, 57, 81, 83, 90, 103, 117
Aley, 76
Alfred, 3, 9, 10, 12, 17, 19, 21, 26, 39, 43, 49, 50, 53, 56, 58, 76, 78, 87, 90, 95, 103, 105, 106, 109, 111, 112

Alfred Turner, 97
Alice, 4, 6, 8, 18, 21, 23, 28, 33,
    34, 36, 50, 51, 65, 103
Allen, 2, 22, 33, 34, 39, 57, 64,
    81, 88, 89, 104, 105, 117;
    James, 3
ALLEN, 85; Catherine A.S.,
    72; E.L., 69; Elizabeth S.,
    72, 85; Fielding A.S., 72, 96
Allis, 95
Allison, 52
Allison Taylor, 92
Allister, 28
Alnusa, 20
Alsey, 21, 48, 72, 78, 87, 97
Alvina, 18
Amanas, 23
Amanda, 2, 3, 7, 10, 12, 16, 17,
    18, 19, 20, 21, 22, 25, 28, 29,
    33, 34, 37, 41, 45, 54, 55, 56,
    58, 59, 60, 64, 67, 68, 69, 71,
    75, 77, 85, 87, 91, 107, 108,
    117
Amanda Ensor, 92
Amanda Ensor Jr., 92
Amanda Melvina, 119
AMBLER: Mary, 113
Ambra, 17
Ambrose, 10, 27, 49, 79
Amelia, 1, 3, 4, 10, 58, 65, 78,
    83, 97, 113, 116
Amelia Cheek, 78
America, 6
Aminta, 18, 92
Amos, 2, 12, 21, 66, 72, 84,
    101, 110
Amos Odell, 109
Amy, 4, 10, 21, 92, 99
Anabelle, 5
Anderson, 2, 79
ANDERSON: Eli, 49; Nancy,
    49
Anderson Corum, 92
Andeson, 23
Andeson Jackson, 16

Andrew, 2, 7, 10, 22, 39, 42,
    48, 56, 77, 88, 92, 114
Andrew Butler, 48
Angelina, 21, 42, 88, 92, 103,
    104
Angeline, 12, 21, 34, 89
Ann, 2, 3, 4, 5, 8, 10, 18, 20,
    24, 27, 28, 29, 30, 33, 34, 37,
    40, 42, 44, 46, 48, 49, 52, 54,
    55, 56, 59, 62, 63, 65, 69, 70,
    72, 78, 79, 81, 84, 91, 92, 95,
    98, 99, 102, 105, 106, 110,
    111, 114
Ann Birch, 78
Ann Eliza, 38, 53
Ann Lightfoot, 92
Ann Maria, 1, 26, 34, 95
Ann Melissa, 40
Anna, 16, 27, 41, 46, 53, 58, 59,
    64, 68, 81, 84, 87, 88, 89, 91,
    102, 110, 115
Anna Eliza, 21
Anna Ensor, 92
Anna Maria, 87
Anne, 22, 76, 82, 112
Annfield, 31, 44, 104
Annie, 5, 8, 18, 29, 70, 99
Annie Moore Warner, 116
Annis, 3
Annmaria, 110
Anthony, 3, 11, 16, 17, 22, 24,
    25, 27, 28, 35, 36, 43, 45, 46,
    48, 49, 52, 55, 58, 59, 62, 68,
    70, 73, 74, 79, 83, 91, 96,
    108, 112
Antony Brent, 79
Araminta, 42
Arch, 2, 22, 30, 34, 41, 52, 106
Archie Coates, 30
Archy, 41, 84
Armistead, 3, 4, 10, 17, 20, 26,
    35, 36, 38, 43, 49, 56, 62, 77,
    84, 90, 92, 99, 107, 117, 119
ARMISTEAD: Bettie Franck,
    107; Bowles E., 107;

Elizabeth, 107; Franck S., 107; Robert L., 23; Walker K., 18
Armistead Parker, 92
Arthur, 1, 2, 3, 17, 18, 20, 29, 37, 38, 39, 41, 45, 54, 55, 57, 58, 59, 60, 64, 68, 69, 81, 97, 99, 102, 104, 107, 117
Arthur Lee, 80
Arthur Smith, 92
Asberry, 78, 105
Asbury, 103
Ash: Jack, 9
Ashby, 11, 12
ASHBY: G.H., 24; Isabella, 21; Mary, 99
Ashley, 3
ASHTON: Ann A., 48, 49; Henry W., 45
Atty, 37
Atwell, 49, 77, 82
Augustine, 54
Austin, 54, 55, 66, 101
AYER: R., 77
Ayers, 95
AYERS: C.R., 117; Charles R., 94; Charles Rufus, 95; Mary W., 21

B_arns, 12
BAER Jr.: Robert, 23
BAILEY: James W., 113; Mary B., 84; Nancy, 111; S.T., 46; Sallie, 110; Samuel, 43, 84
BAILLIS: Sally Ann, 89; Sarah M., 88
BAKER: Mary E., 64; William, 24, 37, 61, 81, 117
Ball: Wilson, 85
BALL: Athelin, 67; Benjamin P., 47; James, 111; Jno, 69; Jno L., 68; John, 67; Joseph, 111; Letty, 111; William, 56, 111

BALTHROPE: Charles A., 24; D.H., 69; Maryan Margaret, 24
BANNEN: Amand B., 112
BARBEE: Mary, 11
BARBER: Thomas, 23
BARBOUR: Elizabeth S., 31; John E., 31; Samuel B., 31
BARKER: Thomas, 23
Barnell, 95
BARNELL, 95
Barnett, 5
Barrett, 84
Bartlett, 68, 69
BARTLETT: Burgess D., 26; Sarah Ann, 26
Bartley, 19, 33, 58, 59
BASEY, 20
BASHAW: Elijah, 111; Robert, 19, 111
Battaile, 103
Bayliss, 23, 65
BAYLISS: Martha C.B., 104; Martha C.G., 30, 39, 57, 79, 81, 105, 117
Baylor, 55
BAYLOR: Ann D., 102, 117, 119; Anne, 105
Beale, 114
BEALE, 77; D.H.C., 119; Giles C., 94; Ludwell D., 110
BEARD: Jonathan, 56
Beck, 23
Becka, 57
BECKHAM: John G., 48
Bell, 117; John, 103
BELL: John N., 23; Sarah, 47, 50, 61
Belle, 103
Belle Lightfoot, 92
Bellila, 58
Ben, 2, 3, 6, 16, 18, 20, 23, 26, 27, 30, 40, 47, 57, 63, 66, 70, 77, 84, 91, 95, 99, 101, 106, 108, 110, 113, 114, 115

Ben Henderson, 79
Ben Tolbert, 3
BENEAR: Henry, 36; Henry H., 38; Mary L., 36
Benjamin, 8, 9, 22, 23, 27, 47, 66, 69, 83, 91, 98, 100, 108
Benjamin Corum, 92
BENNETT: Alexander H., 87; Almira J., 87; Frances, 87; Isabella C., 87; Laura Roberta, 87; Mary E., 87; Minerva, 111
Bennley: Aaron, 44; Lewis, 44; Olley, 44; Strother, 44
Bentley, 87
Benton, 61, 80, 97
Berry: Jane, 78
Berryman, 58, 59, 68
Bert Lightfoot, 92
Betsy, 5, 19, 23, 37, 45, 60, 65, 66, 68, 77, 78, 81, 84, 85, 88, 90, 96, 97, 103, 105, 107, 110
Betsy Mason, 94
Betty, 2, 4, 7, 12, 19, 23, 25, 50, 51, 55, 66, 69, 70, 71, 72, 80, 81, 82, 84, 88, 93, 97, 103, 110, 111, 119
Betty Ann, 2
Betty Leonard, 4
Beverly, 2, 7, 22, 34, 39, 47, 48, 52, 57, 63, 71, 77, 79, 81, 93, 96, 97, 104, 111, 117
BEVERLY: Jane, 116; Robert, 46
Beverly Lake, 90
BIGGS: Nancy E., 60
Bill, 17, 18, 20, 35, 45, 53, 56, 58, 59, 68, 69, 80, 93, 101, 107, 108, 114, 120
Billy, 3, 9, 15, 17, 26, 30, 42, 48, 49, 56, 61, 66, 70, 84, 88, 89, 95, 97, 103, 104, 105, 110
Billy Blackwell, 3

Billy Burk, 118
Billy Fox, 119, 120
Billy Jr., 49, 103
Billy Peyton, 3
Billy Sr., 49
Billy Warner, 95
Birch: Ann, 78
Birky, 113
BLACKMAN: Mrs., 12
BLACKMORE: Julia E., 57
BLACKNILL: James, 23
Blacksmith: Jasper, 4; Jim, 4; Page, 4
Blackwell, 80; Billy, 3; Ellen, 92; Lucy, 3
BLACKWELL: Arthur, 38; B., 46, 68; Elizabeth, 102, 115; Elizabeth P., 90, 92; Ella, 89; Emily G., 2; Emma, 89; Gen. John, 2; Hannah R., 89; James, 23; Jno E., 89; John E., 2, 89; Lucy F., 2; Margaret, 38; Margaret B., 57; P., 69
Bland, 6
Bob, 4, 6, 17, 20, 41, 52, 53, 54, 55, 56, 67, 70, 76, 78, 80, 89, 92, 93, 99, 103, 104, 106, 111, 114, 115, 116, 121
BOGGESS: Nancy, 107; Nancy E., 42, 48, 78, 91, 117
Bonaparte, 9
BONSETT: Mary T., 12; Simon, 12
BOOKE: Martin P., 109
Booker, 64
Boss: Harriet, 78
BOSWELL: Mary F., 11
BOTCLER: Edward, 72, 80; Joseph, 29, 49, 97; Nancy G., 72
BOTCLER Jr.: Sarah, 49
BOTTS: Thornton S., 120
BOWEN: Albinia, 25; Ellen, 113; William A., 41

Calphus, 81
Calvin, 39
Camilla, 37
CAMPBELL: James H., 23
Carey, 47
Caroline, 3, 11, 12, 16, 17, 20,
    21, 23, 31, 37, 40, 41, 42, 44,
    47, 48, 51, 52, 54, 56, 57, 58,
    59, 60, 64, 66, 67, 68, 72, 75,
    76, 80, 85, 87, 90, 93, 94,
    101, 103, 104, 105, 106, 107,
    108, 111, 112
Caroline Picket, 85
CARR: Caldwell, 64; John, 77;
    Louisa Cornelia, 64
Carter, 2, 7, 20, 54, 56, 65, 67,
    92, 99, 102, 103, 115; Milly,
    95; Phillip, 79
CARTER: A.R., 70; George,
    40, 62, 108, 109; J.H., 48;
    Oaird W. Combs, 7; Sarah
    C., 120; Thomas O.B., 62
CARVER: Catherine O. White,
    71; William, 6
Cass, 24
Cassiopeia, 19
Cassius, 71, 87
Cate, 22
Cath, 120
Catharine, 66, 76, 79, 90, 93,
    95, 113
Catharine Marshall, 21
Catherine, 3, 5, 6, 24, 33, 38,
    42, 50, 51, 57, 58, 59, 61, 72,
    75, 76, 88, 90, 99, 100, 101,
    103, 108, 113
CAYNOR: James, 26, 33; John,
    26, 33; William, 26, 33
Ceanna, 36
Cecelia, 19
Cecil, 120
Cecilia, 47
Cecily, 3
Cela, 81, 111

Celia, 3, 19, 27, 31, 44, 46, 58,
    59, 63, 65, 66, 69, 81, 91, 92,
    103, 104, 114, 115, 116
Celia Ann Jackson, 92
Celia Campbell, 112
Celia Jr., 46, 63, 70, 83, 91, 115
Celia Sr., 63, 83, 91, 115, 116
Cely, 33, 101
Cesar, 22
Cetty, 36
Chaney Love, 62
Chantel, 20
Chapman, 97, 102; Albert, 92;
    Hendley, 92; Jane, 92; Lucy,
    3
Charity, 30, 53, 83, 84
Charles, 2, 4, 6, 7, 9, 10, 15, 17,
    18, 20, 22, 28, 29, 33, 34, 38,
    39, 40, 44, 48, 49, 50, 51, 53,
    54, 57, 60, 62, 63, 64, 66, 68,
    69, 70, 76, 78, 79, 81, 84, 85,
    87, 90, 92, 93, 95, 96, 97, 99,
    101, 102, 103, 104, 105, 106,
    110, 111, 114, 117, 118, 120
Charles Alexander, 40
Charles Brockley, 17
Charles Brown, 27
Charles Bruce, 17
Charles Buckle, 27
Charles Butler, 48, 92
Charles Fox, 92
Charles Henry, 97
Charles Jr., 66
Charles Sr., 66
Charles Stuart, 92
Charlotte, 2, 3, 4, 7, 10, 18, 19,
    20, 22, 25, 30, 31, 33, 37, 42,
    47, 48, 50, 52, 54, 55, 56, 57,
    65, 66, 67, 76, 81, 85, 89, 95,
    101, 102, 104, 105, 107, 114,
    117
Chartal, 20
Chasity, 30
Chass, 95
Cheek: Amelia, 78; Bristoe, 78

111; Lindsey, 6; Lizza Taylor, 92; Louisa Johnson, 92; Lucy, 57; Lucy Corum, 92; Lucy Graves, 92; Lucy Jackson, 110; Major, 110; Margaret, 11; Maria, 92, 110; Maria Parker, 92; Martha Burress, 92; Martin, 99; Martin Jr., 98, 99; Martin Sr., 98; Mary, 57, 66, 99, 111; Mary Fletcher, 92, 94; Mary Jackson, 92; Mary Turner, 11; Melinda, 98, 102; Milly Washington, 92; Milton Taylor, 92; Moses S__ell, 67; Nancy, 43; Obid Duncan, 92; Patsy, 57; Peter, 11, 98, 99; Priscilla, 98; Richard, 98; Sally, 11, 57, 94; Samuel, 98; Sandy, 92; Sarah Ann Lightfoot, 92; Sary Frances, 11; Scike, 99; Shadrack, 98, 99; Sophia, 30; Susan, 98; Susan Jackson, 92; Tamar, 92; Tamer Butler, 92; Taylor Jackson, 92; Thornton Taylor, 92; Tristan, 51; Vernon Butler, 92; Vianna, 11, 94; Violet, 92; Violet Stuart, 92; Waverly Corum, 92; Wellford Butler, 92; Wesley, 45; Wiley, 51; William, 88, 98, 99; William Henry Burress, 92; Willie Ann Corum, 92

Emanuel, 20, 29, 89, 118

Embrey, 48

EMBREY: Elizabeth V., 33, 46, 61, 76; Frederick, 90; George W., 33, 46, 61; John, 46; John L., 76; John S., 33; John T., 60, 107; Judson G., 33; Judson I., 46, 76; Judson J., 60, 61; Judson S., 33;

Lucinda, 33; Oswald P., 90; Robert, 79, 89; Robert D., 90; Sarah, 79, 90; Stanton G., 90; Susan I., 46, 76; Susan J., 33; Thomas, 19, 33, 35; Wilford, 33; Wilford S., 61, 76; Wilfred S., 46; William, 95

Emeline, 6, 66, 83

Emily, 1, 2, 3, 18, 19, 20, 22, 25, 26, 29, 33, 34, 37, 38, 39, 42, 45, 50, 52, 57, 58, 59, 60, 67, 68, 69, 71, 76, 77, 81, 84, 85, 88, 94, 103, 104, 107, 108, 109, 114

Emily Bumbey, 53

Emily Taylor, 92

Emma, 1, 26, 49, 77, 97, 103

Emmanuel, 117

Emmet, 114

Emmett, 104, 110

Emory, 53

EMRY: Robert, 88

Ennis, 47

Enoch, 3, 19, 28, 31, 33, 34, 61, 76, 93

Ensor: Amanda, 92; Anna, 92; Edney, 92; Eliza, 92; Laura, 92

ENSOR: Jemima, 36

Ensor Jr.: Amanda, 92

Ephraim, 18, 20, 23, 27, 46, 63, 70, 83, 91, 107, 115, 118

Ernest, 118

Esau, 107

Esilinaha, 23

ESKRIDGE: Alexander W., 117; Andrew J., 33, 51, 53; Bernard L., 117; Harriet, 35; James, 33, 35; Julia A., 33; Julia Ann, 51; Monroe, 117; Rodham, 117, 119; Samuel L., 33

Esther, 3, 42, 103

EUSTACE: Adalade, 4; James, 4; John, 4, 5; Louisa Josephine, 4; Louisa R., 4; Phillip C., 42; Sarah L.C., 42; Susan James, 4; William H., 42

Evaline, 38

Evan, 7

Evans, 7

Eve, 21, 30, 50, 88, 94, 97

Evelina, 23, 31, 50, 58, 59, 62, 77, 95, 97, 106, 108, 109, 110

Evelina Bumbey, 53

Eveline, 39, 40, 49, 97, 101, 114, 119

Even, 107

EVENS: Margaret H., 100

F_rida, 57

Fanny, 3, 4, 7, 8, 9, 11, 12, 16, 17, 18, 20, 21, 22, 25, 27, 28, 31, 33, 36, 37, 39, 40, 41, 42, 45, 46, 52, 54, 58, 59, 62, 63, 64, 65, 66, 68, 69, 70, 71, 72, 78, 79, 80, 81, 82, 84, 91, 94, 95, 96, 98, 103, 106, 107, 109, 110, 111, 115, 116, 119

Fanny Bumbey, 53

Fanny Ferguson, 62

Fanny Grandson, 40

Fanny Johnson, 92

Fanny Lee, 113

Fanny Warner, 116

FANT: Jno M., 69

FARION: George A., 18

FARROW: George A., 18

FAUNT: John L., 114

Fayette, 56

FEAGANS: Benjamin, 11, 81; Daniel, 11, 19, 81; Elizabeth, 24; Fanny, 11, 81; Hannah, 81; John, 11, 19, 26; John R., 11, 81

Felicia, 2, 22, 45

Felix, 49, 82

Felix Taylor, 92

FELTON: Mary, 11; William H., 11

Fenley, 2, 76

Fenton, 43, 50, 77, 78, 88, 92, 99, 100, 103, 106

Ferguson: Fanny, 62; Robert, 95

FERGUSON: John D., 100, 102; Josiah, 19

Festus Grant, 92

FICKLIN: A.S., 6, 63, 77, 79; Anthony, 90; Anthony S., 22, 29, 39, 52, 96; Virginia, 98; William P., 40, 63

Fielden, 107

Fielding, 114

FISHBACK: Jno A., 26; Josiah T., 30; Martha Jane, 26; Nancy, 26; Nelson N., 26; Sarah Ann, 26; Sarah T., 26

Fisher: James A., 55

FISHER: Capt. Thomas, 52; Dade, 55; Elias, 55; Elizabeth, 40; Francis, 55; George L., 55; James A., 55; Jno, 55; John, 55; Martha A., 55; Martha Ann, 51; Mary E., 55; Richard, 55; Robert, 55; Samuel, 55; Sarah M., 55; Thomas, 51, 54, 55, 74; Thomas H., 55; William G., 55

Fitia, 42

FITZHOUGH: Abby Mays, 95; Bella, 96; George Warren, 95; Lucy B., 96; Thomas L., 96

FITZHUGH: George T., 113; Giles, 40; Henry, 113; Lucy B., 42, 83; Martha S., 120; Sally R., 113; Thomas, 113

Fleet, 2

Fleming, 48, 111

Fleming Jordan, 48
Fletcher: Mary, 92, 94
FLETCHER: Catherine, 54; E.W., 61; Elias W., 50, 54, 56, 65, 77, 80, 98, 114; John G., 66, 99, 114; Robert, 61; William, 68
FLETCHER Jr.: Joshua, 54, 61; William, 61
Florence, 25, 75
Florida, 97
Florinza Sowers, 92
FLOWERREE: Contee, 52, 77; Eliza E., 52; Judy, 52
FOLEY: E.H., 101; Eliza, 6; Elizabeth, 6, 18, 36; Kitty, 18; Nancy, 18; Sally, 18; William, 18
FOLLIN: M.J., 48
FOOTE: Frances T., 120
FORBES: J.M., 115
FOSTER: Susan A., 41, 50
FOUK: E., 23
Fountain, 80
Fox: Billy, 119, 120; Charles, 92
FOX: James H., 68; John, 114
Frances, 1, 2, 3, 7, 8, 9, 13, 18, 19, 20, 22, 24, 25, 29, 34, 39, 40, 47, 51, 52, 55, 57, 61, 65, 75, 81, 84, 93, 103, 115
Francis, 45, 49, 50, 52, 55, 57, 71, 75, 83, 90, 107, 108, 120
Frank, 2, 5, 8, 15, 17, 18, 27, 35, 37, 46, 49, 53, 56, 57, 58, 59, 63, 68, 69, 70, 81, 82, 84, 88, 91, 95, 98, 100, 102, 106, 107, 109, 111, 115, 116, 117
Franklin, 76, 87
FRANKLIN: Lucy J., 5
Franky, 16, 17, 19, 22, 28, 36, 45, 53, 61, 88
FRAZIER: Caroline Eliza, 64

Frederick, 2, 4, 7, 8, 22, 39, 52, 57, 58, 64, 68, 69, 81, 84, 85, 88, 90, 100, 104, 105
Frederick Thomson, 92
Fredrick, 34, 89
FREEMAN: James, 68; William A., 108
FRENCH: James, 44, 53; James H., 31, 44, 104; Janius B., 31, 44, 103; Marcellus, 31, 44; Matilda, 31; Matilda C., 44; Rosalie, 44; Rosalie H., 31, 103

G__LY: William, 23
Gabriel, 7, 25, 33, 52, 58, 76, 78, 103
GACKINS: Mary, 106
GAINES: Amanda, 55; Edwin, 48; Elizabeth S., 55; Harriet, 55; John, 56; Lucian, 56; Mrs. M.C., 55; R.H., 56; Richard H., 54, 55, 70; Virginia, 56; William, 56; William H., 46, 48
Garret, 21
Garrett, 102
Garrison, 17
GASKINS: Henry, 17
General, 96
George, 1, 2, 3, 4, 5, 7, 8, 10, 11, 12, 16, 17, 18, 20, 22, 23, 24, 25, 26, 27, 28, 29, 30, 31, 33, 34, 36, 37, 38, 39, 40, 42, 45, 46, 47, 48, 49, 50, 51, 52, 53, 54, 56, 57, 58, 59, 60, 61, 64, 65, 66, 68, 69, 72, 76, 77, 78, 79, 81, 82, 84, 85, 88, 92, 93, 94, 95, 96, 97, 99, 101, 103, 104, 107, 108, 111, 112, 114, 115, 117, 120, 121; Thomas, 21
GEORGE: Aleshia P., 25; B., 25; Benjamin, 25; Benjamin P., 111; Bernard, 25, 111,

103

HALLEY: Dr. Samuel H., 45
Ham, 68, 69, 120
Hamilton, 58, 61
HAMILTON: J.L., 68, 69;
  Lavinia T., 97; Lavinia Y.,
  95
Hamson, 69
Hanley, 3
Hannah, 1, 2, 5, 6, 9, 10, 12, 15,
  16, 20, 21, 24, 26, 27, 28, 30,
  34, 41, 46, 50, 52, 54, 56, 58,
  59, 63, 64, 68, 70, 76, 82, 84,
  88, 91, 94, 96, 97, 98, 101,
  107, 109, 111, 115, 116
Hannah Payne, 62
Hanner, 4
Hannibal, 57
HANSBROUGH: David, 15,
  18; Elijah, 15, 18, 20, 29;
  Hiram, 18; James, 18;
  Jonathan, 18; Mary W., 8;
  Peter, 19, 29; Phineas, 18;
  Samuel, 18
HARDING: Angeline, 63;
  Strother, 21
Harriet, 1, 3, 4, 7, 8, 10, 12, 16,
  17, 18, 19, 20, 21, 26, 30, 31,
  33, 34, 37, 38, 39, 44, 45, 47,
  48, 49, 50, 51, 53, 54, 56, 58,
  60, 61, 64, 66, 68, 69, 72, 75,
  76, 81, 84, 88, 89, 90, 93, 95,
  100, 101, 103, 104, 105, 106,
  107, 108, 112, 113
Harriet Boss, 78
Harriet Gibson, 78
Harris, 58, 59, 68
Harris Grant, 114
Harrison, 2, 18, 19, 20, 22, 28,
  36, 50, 53, 61, 66, 67, 71, 81,
  99
HARRISON: Thomas G., 12
Harry, 20, 22, 42, 56, 66, 67,
  69, 70, 76, 78, 80, 84, 91,
  105, 111
Harry Reid, 114

Harry Welk, 17
HART: Catherine, 48; Robert,
  48
Hartman, 80, 87, 93
HATCHER: Gourley M., 34;
  Gourley R., 19
Hatty Maria, 6
Haydon, 84
HAYNIE: Martha, 34; Martha
  H., 2, 22, 57
Haywood, 2, 18, 82
Hedgman, 27, 47, 63, 70, 83,
  91, 114, 115, 116
HEFFELBOWER: Mary
  Evelina, 47
HEFLIN: William, 68, 69
Helen, 72
HELM: Erasmus, 18; James, 9;
  Joannah, 8; Jon, 9; Lena, 84;
  Lina, 9; Margaret, 9;
  Richard, 9; Thomas, 8, 9;
  William, 107
Henderson, 4, 11, 18, 40, 114;
  Ben, 79
Hendley Chapman, 92
HENDON: Margaret, 68
Henley, 66
Henrietta, 7, 50, 88, 89, 107,
  108
Henry, 1, 2, 3, 5, 7, 8, 9, 10, 11,
  12, 15, 16, 17, 18, 19, 20, 22,
  23, 24, 25, 27, 29, 30, 31, 33,
  38, 39, 41, 42, 44, 45, 47, 48,
  49, 50, 52, 53, 54, 55, 56, 57,
  58, 59, 60, 61, 63, 64, 65, 67,
  68, 69, 71, 72, 73, 76, 77, 80,
  81, 82, 83, 84, 85, 86, 87, 88,
  90, 92, 94, 95, 96, 97, 99,
  100, 103, 104, 105, 107, 109,
  114, 117, 118, 119
Henry Brooke, 15
Henry Butler, 48
Henry C. Johnson, 85
Henry Clay, 30
Henry Corum, 92

Henry Gibson, 46, 63, 70, 82, 91, 115, 116
Henry Jackson, 46
Henry Lansdown, 53
Henry Miller, 46, 70, 82, 91, 115
Henry Millon, 63
Henry Wager, 90
Henry Wills, 27
Henson, 3, 25, 85, 90
Hercules, 27, 70, 83, 91, 115, 116
HERNDON: Margaret E., 80; Traverse D., 53
Herron, 92
Hester, 7, 8, 29, 55, 110
Hester Ann, 78
Hetty, 57
HICKS: Ann M., 69; Emma, 67, 69; I.A., 69; Mary N., 69; Stephen G., 77
HICKS Jr.: Kimble, 51
HICKS Sr.: K.G., 51
Hierochaler, 33
HILL: Horace B., 109; Lucy, 109, 116
HINSON: George W., 1; Susan, 111
HIRST: Thompson M., 91, 94
HITCH: John, 6
HITT: Fanny, 54; Mariah, 72; Peter A., 54; Polly, 54; Reuben, 54; William, 72
HOGE: Joshua, 53, 70; Mary, 70
HOLDEN: Jane, 111
HOLMES: Elizabeth, 11; James S., 78, 88
HOLTZCLAW: Charles, 7, 17, 26; Eli, 40; Elizabeth, 7, 11; Frances, 7, 101
Hopkins: James, 92
HOPPER: Mary, 35

Horace, 2, 7, 33, 45, 51, 67, 80, 83, 87, 90, 93, 97, 101, 108, 120
HORD: Ambrose, 72; Charity, 54; Enos, 72; William, 72
HORNER: Ann, 26; Anna Maria, 100; Barbara L., 34, 45, 60; Emily, 34, 60; Iman, 100, 119; Inman, 102; William, 100
HOVE: Dade, 66; Henry, 66; Howson, 66; John, 66; Mrs., 66; Robert H., 66
Howard, 3, 20, 21, 52, 55, 58, 59, 69, 103
Hudnall, 97
HUDNALL: Albert, 13, 29; Alexander, 30; James, 30
Hugh, 23, 54, 55
Hulda, 116
HUME: Benjamin L., 26; Charles E., 63, 70, 82, 91, 115, 116; Elizabeth, 26, 28, 38; John W., 51; Margaret, 51, 55, 67; Margaret M., 45; Mary, 70, 82; Mary E., 46, 63, 91
Humphrey, 47, 48, 56, 62, 64, 65, 77, 97, 98, 99, 112, 121
HUMPHREY: Jane, 110
HUNT: Thomas H., 34
HUNTON: Charles, 47, 48; Elizabeth C., 77; Frances E., 27; Gen. Eppa, 67; Silas B., 27; William, 9; William G., 66
HUTCHINSON: Alexander, 16, 37, 41, 75; Cornelia, 16, 37, 75; Cynthia, 16, 37, 41, 76; Edgar, 16, 37; Edgar S., 75; Maria, 16, 41, 75; Reuben, 16, 37, 65, 72, 75
HUTCHISON: Beverly, 116

IDEN: Eliza, 8; Elizabeth, 7, 80; Manaly, 8
Iman, 52
Indiana, 95, 97
Inman, 55
Irene, 49
Isaac, 3, 7, 12, 18, 27, 34, 45, 52, 57, 58, 72, 83, 84, 85, 88, 89, 94, 98, 105, 106, 109
Isaac Brent, 79
Isabell, 72
ISABELL: Mary, 112, 120; Sarah Ann W., 8
Isabella, 18, 20, 39, 80, 113
Isadora, 40
Isaiah, 27
Isaiah Parker, 92
Isham, 78
Israel, 19, 41, 78
Isy, 95

Jack, 1, 3, 9, 11, 18, 19, 20, 23, 24, 29, 31, 33, 46, 49, 52, 54, 57, 58, 59, 60, 66, 67, 68, 69, 70, 71, 73, 84, 91, 95, 97, 106, 109, 113, 114, 118, 119
Jack Ash, 9
Jack Jones, 17, 27
Jackson, 6, 18, 20, 22, 27, 29, 39, 41, 46, 52, 57, 63, 70, 82, 91, 110, 113, 115, 116, 118; Albert, 92; Andeson, 16; Celia Ann, 92; Henry, 46; Lucy, 110; Mary, 92; Susan, 92; Taylor, 92
JACKSON: Anne E., 116; George, 15; Harriet V., 116; John F., 75; Willard L., 116
Jacob, 6, 12, 21, 34, 47, 51, 57, 63, 78, 88, 90, 94, 115
Jacob Frederick, 6
Jake, 97, 115, 120
James, 2, 3, 10, 11, 16, 18, 21, 23, 26, 27, 30, 31, 33, 37, 38, 39, 42, 44, 45, 49, 51, 52, 62, 64, 65, 68, 69, 73, 82, 84, 85, 88, 90, 93, 95, 97, 98, 101, 104, 108, 113, 119, 120; Lewis, 80; Phoebe, 89
JAMES, 57; A., 69; Aldridge, 106; Benjamin, 57; Fleming, 106; J.W., 106; Jane, 119; John T., 77, 106; Joseph, 82; Judson, 18; Mahlen, 94; Marshall K., 106; Mary Ann, 57; Sallie, 113, 120; Sarah E., 99, 121; Susan G., 77
James Allen, 3
James Custis, 99
James Henry, 103
James Henry Taylor, 92
James Hopkins, 92
James Madison, 76
James William, 70
Jane, 2, 3, 4, 7, 11, 12, 16, 19, 20, 22, 23, 25, 27, 28, 29, 33, 34, 35, 36, 38, 39, 42, 45, 47, 48, 51, 53, 58, 59, 61, 63, 64, 66, 71, 72, 75, 78, 81, 83, 85, 88, 93, 95, 96, 97, 98, 99, 101, 106, 107, 113, 116, 117, 119, 120
Jane Berry, 78
Jane Chapman, 92
Jane Frances, 12
Jane Lawdy, 78
Jane Payne, 94, 118
Janet, 114
Jannette Warner, 116
Janny, 49
Jared, 84
Jarrett, 2, 97, 109
Jarrett Jackson, 100
Jasper Blacksmith, 4
Jeannette, 88
JEBBETS: Hannah, 104
Jeff, 4, 18, 20, 27, 63, 88, 90, 93, 94; William, 83, 115
Jefferson, 2, 10, 15, 68, 80
Jeffrey, 17, 19

Jeffries, 77

JEFFRIES: Agatha, 65; Agnes, 54, 65, 76; Eli, 92; Elizabeth, 92; Enoch, 64; Eustace, 64; George, 92; James E., 17, 31; John, 64, 92; John B., 23; Joseph, 64; Josephine, 64; Josephine M., 31, 50, 61, 77; Lemuel, 92; Nancy, 8; Paisley N., 8; Presley N., 54

Jemima, 19, 20, 107

Jemmy, 84

Jennie, 115

JENNINGS: Fannie, 107; I.L., 68; Jemima, 4; Lewis, 4; Lewis T.L., 70; Lucinda, 70, 79; Virginia B., 83

Jenny, 7, 24, 37, 45, 49, 51, 58, 59, 67, 68, 69, 75, 80, 88, 90, 93, 94, 96, 97, 104, 106, 116, 117, 120

Jenny Stuart, 92

Jeremiah, 16, 72

Jeremy, 17

Jerry, 2, 3, 16, 41, 42, 56, 58, 64, 67, 75, 84, 93, 95, 97, 101, 113, 118

Jerry Moore, 84

Jesse, 3, 4, 10, 25, 30, 36, 37, 40, 41, 42, 49, 50, 66, 71, 77, 110, 120

Jesse McClintock, 21

Jesse Strother, 62

Jeter, 50

JETT: Francis M., 91, 94, 105; William H., 72

Jillson, 119

Jilson, 39

Jim, 3, 8, 10, 12, 16, 21, 22, 24, 25, 26, 37, 39, 41, 50, 52, 54, 58, 59, 63, 64, 65, 72, 75, 77, 78, 79, 84, 85, 88, 89, 93, 94, 96, 97, 101, 103, 107, 119, 120

Jim Blacksmith, 4

Jim Clow, 65

Jinny, 41, 60, 64, 66, 81, 89, 94, 103, 106, 107

Jno, 65

Jno Lucas, 104

Jno Robert, 30

Jno Scott, 89

Jo, 50

Joan, 6, 97

Joanna, 38, 39

Joe, 5, 7, 9, 10, 12, 19, 21, 25, 30, 35, 42, 45, 51, 52, 54, 55, 63, 70, 71, 75, 77, 78, 79, 81, 87, 90, 93, 95, 96, 97, 101, 103, 104, 106, 108, 109, 113, 114, 120

Joe Chum, 115

Joe Lake, 90

John, 1, 2, 3, 4, 6, 7, 10, 11, 13, 15, 17, 18, 19, 20, 21, 22, 23, 24, 25, 26, 27, 29, 31, 33, 34, 35, 37, 38, 39, 42, 44, 45, 46, 47, 48, 49, 50, 51, 52, 53, 54, 55, 56, 57, 58, 59, 61, 62, 65, 66, 67, 71, 72, 75, 76, 77, 81, 82, 83, 87, 91, 94, 97, 99, 102, 103, 104, 105, 107, 108, 109, 112, 114, 116

JOHN: Nancy, 24

John Bell, 103

John Brown, 103

John Clow, 65

John Henry, 103

John Love, 62

John Lucas, 95, 115

John Mauzy, 92

John Roberts, 48

John Scott, 114

John Titus, 85

John William Burrus, 92

John Wood, 71, 109

Johnny, 115

Johnson, 25, 78, 92, 99; Betty, 92; David, 92; Delia, 92; Edwin, 92; Fanny, 92;

Greenly, 92; Henry C., 85;
Louisa, 92
JOHNSON: Amelia, 15;
Elizabeth, 11; Joseph, 91;
Moses, 1, 99; Presley, 11;
Smith, 11; Susan, 41, 99;
Thomas, 68; Thomas Y., 88,
90
Jonah, 97
Jonas, 61
Jones: Jack, 17
JONES: Braudas, 84; Charles,
18, 43; Elizabeth, 9; Emily
Ann, 35; James S., 35; John,
18; Mary, 8; Thomas, 85,
109; W.T., 84; William, 34;
William R., 97, 119
Jordan: Fleming, 48; Samuel,
48
Joseph, 2, 18, 20, 22, 24, 30,
38, 42, 49, 55, 66, 75, 87, 89,
92
Joseph Butler, 120
Josephine, 50, 84, 95, 103
Joshua, 10, 60, 64, 99, 116
Josiah, 37
Juda, 3, 8, 19, 110
Judah, 65, 66
Jude, 98
Judea, 52
Judge, 39
Judith, 3, 4, 34, 54, 55
Judson, 50
Judy, 7, 10, 17, 20, 35, 38, 42,
43, 50, 52, 53, 65, 66, 71, 73,
79, 83, 84, 87, 91, 96, 101,
102, 109
Judy Clow, 64
Judy Jr., 71, 91, 109
Judy Sr., 109
Judy Warner, 62
Julia, 2, 18, 19, 20, 25, 29, 45,
72, 80, 87, 88, 97, 98, 103,
108, 110, 119
Julia Ann, 78

Julia Ann Burress, 92
Julian, 78
Julianna, 16, 22, 25
Julie, 89
Juliet, 3, 30, 49, 55, 81, 82, 93,
98, 99, 105, 107
Julius, 19, 42, 81; Peter, 117
Julius Parker, 92
July, 41
Juston, 10

Kane, 100
Kate, 95, 96, 111
Kayse, 106
KEITH: Alexander D., 45;
James, 6; Judith, 77
KELLY: Jesse, 79
Kelura, 19
Kemp, 3, 4, 24, 39, 101
Kemper, 2, 34, 57, 81, 104, 117
KEMPER: Alexander H., 69;
Alexander Hamilton, 69;
Alice, 69; George, 69, 80,
87, 93; H.F., 69, 80, 87;
Henry, 93; Henry F., 81,
101; John M., 96; Joshua,
11, 28; Julia Ann, 80; Juliet
Ann, 69; Lucy, 69; P., 87;
Peter, 80, 87; Rosamond, 72;
Samuel, 68, 80, 87
Kenton, 28
Kepsie, 69
KERCHEVAL: Elijah, 51
KERTON: Frances, 5
Keturah, 81
Keziah, 1, 16, 18, 26, 31, 44,
51, 53, 75, 90, 93, 101, 103,
104, 108
KIETH: Marshall, 27
KINCHELOE: Ann H., 62;
Conrad B., 62; James M., 62;
John W., 62; Thomas I., 62
Kingston, 45
Kitt, 45

Kitty, 2, 3, 5, 10, 11, 12, 15, 20, 22, 38, 39, 47, 48, 50, 51, 52, 53, 57, 64, 70, 71, 77, 80, 95, 105, 113, 120
Kitty Ann, 58, 59
Kiziah, 75
Kizzy, 58, 59
KLIPSTEIN: Phillip A., 65
KORKMAN, 19

Lake: Beverly, 90; Joe, 90
LAKE, 105; _.E., 34; A., 43; Alvernon J., 104; Dewitt C., 84; Eleanor B., 38, 43; Isaac, 27, 28, 34, 37, 43, 50; L.T.W., 43; Ludwell, 34; R.E., 43; Sara, 99; Sarah Lewis, 41; Thomas M., 34; William, 99
Landon, 3
Landora, 85
Lane: Lewis, 78
Lansdown: Henry, 53
Lara, 110
Larkin, 5
Latham: Lucy, 62
LATHAM: Jane C., 67; Sarah, 90; William, 66
Lauck: Daniel, 90
LAUCK: William E., 78
Laura, 4, 10, 50, 57, 71, 77, 89, 95, 102, 103, 106, 107, 109, 110, 120
Laura Ensor, 92
Laurinda, 7
Lavina, 23, 33, 38, 42
Lavinia, 30, 39, 41, 52, 58, 64, 99, 107
LAWLER: Ann, 110; Mary Ann, 102; Robert A., 102; William, 102, 106
Lawrence, 83, 84
LAWRENCE: Elizabeth M., 8; William O., 8
LAWS: Shadrack, 57, 117

Lawson, 8, 49, 109, 119
Leach, 79
Leah, 102
Leaner, 96
Leanna, 51, 52, 75, 107
LEARY: John, 112; Mrs., 114
Lee, 103, 106, 110; Arthur, 80; Fanny, 113; Lewis, 78
LEE: Fanny, 82; Margaret G., 18
LEITH: Martha, 113
Lemima, 92
Lemmon, 33
Lemon, 114
Lemuel, 35, 88
Lena, 3, 63, 81
Lenis, 18
Leny, 8
Leonard: Betty, 4
Let, 12
Letia, 18, 20
Letitia, 11, 12, 66, 83
Letty, 12, 21, 29, 42, 47, 49, 66, 67, 79, 80, 81, 92, 96, 99, 106, 107
Levi, 50
Levina, 79, 107
Lewellen, 54, 55, 111
Lewellyn, 7, 8, 31, 104, 110
Lewis, 1, 2, 3, 4, 5, 8, 10, 11, 12, 20, 21, 23, 27, 31, 36, 38, 39, 44, 46, 49, 51, 52, 54, 55, 56, 57, 58, 59, 60, 62, 63, 64, 66, 68, 69, 70, 71, 75, 78, 81, 83, 90, 92, 93, 94, 95, 96, 97, 100, 101, 103, 104, 106, 108, 109, 111, 118, 119, 120, 121
LEWIS: Catherine M., 41, 42; Dr. I.R., 68; Fanny A., 82; Henry M., 49, 77; Lucinda, 82; Richard, 73, 82; William H., 73, 82
Lewis Bennley, 44
Lewis James, 80
Lewis Jr., 103

Lewis Keith, 89
Lewis Lane, 78
Lewis Lee, 78
Lewis Seddon, 80
Licia, 22
Liddy, 24, 29, 88
Lidia, 3, 49
Lightfoot: Ann, 92; Belle, 92; Bert, 92; Ida Belle, 92; Sarah Ann, 92
Lila, 64
Lilly, 57, 90, 97, 104, 111
Lilly Butler, 48
Limas, 78
Limas Jr., 78
Lina, 58, 59, 80
Lindsey, 6
Lindy, 101
Liney, 57
Linny, 49, 57
Liss, 6
Littleton, 97
Liza, 5, 20, 66, 113
Lizza, 10
Lizza Taylor, 92
Lizzie, 95, 103, 107, 108, 113, 114, 120
Lizzy, 18, 21, 28, 43, 64, 65, 105
Lloyd, 84, 101
Logan, 23, 51
Lomax: Molly, 62
LOMAX: Eliza, 97; Miriam C., 1, 46; Susan, 1; Thomas M., 84, 97
Long: Lucy, 79
LONG: Robert, 15
LONGHBOROUGH: Caroline J., 64; Nathan, 48
Lorinda, 84
Lorra, 57
Louisa, 4, 5, 10, 15, 18, 20, 22, 23, 25, 28, 34, 39, 49, 51, 53, 56, 58, 59, 68, 69, 71, 82, 93, 101, 110, 112, 114, 119

Louisa Ann, 9
Louisa Johnson, 92
Louisa Jr., 114
Love: Chaney, 62; Dolly, 62; John, 62
LOVE: Col. George, 53; George, 50
LOVELL: Alice T., 26; Mrs. A.T., 29
Lucas: Jno, 104; John, 95
LUCAS: Mrs., 50, 61; Nancy E., 47; Robert Wyndham, 47
Lucia, 39
Lucian, 101
Lucina, 68
Lucinda, 2, 4, 5, 6, 8, 9, 10, 13, 23, 25, 30, 34, 41, 47, 48, 49, 52, 60, 61, 64, 66, 68, 78, 79, 85, 89, 95, 97, 100, 114, 119
Lucindy, 49
Lucius, 15
LUCKETT: Horace, 56; Joanna T., 93; Nancy, 7; Richard, 21, 28; Thomas, 7
Lucy, 1, 2, 3, 4, 6, 8, 9, 10, 16, 18, 19, 20, 22, 23, 25, 27, 28, 29, 30, 33, 34, 36, 39, 41, 42, 44, 45, 46, 47, 49, 50, 52, 54, 55, 57, 58, 59, 61, 62, 63, 64, 65, 66, 67, 70, 71, 76, 77, 79, 82, 85, 90, 91, 94, 95, 96, 97, 102, 103, 105, 106, 107, 110, 111, 113, 115, 117, 118
Lucy Ann, 30, 31, 46, 52, 72
Lucy Blackwell, 3
Lucy Chapman, 3
Lucy Cook, 95
Lucy Corum, 92
Lucy Ellen, 91
Lucy Graves, 92
Lucy Jackson, 110
Lucy Latham, 62
Lucy Long, 79
Lucy Mildred, 96
Lucy Obanion, 85

Lucy Scott, 85
Lucy Taylor, 89
Lucy Walker, 62
Ludwell, 18, 50
LUPTON: Nathaniel C., 23
Lycurgus, 40
Lydia, 6, 50, 84, 101, 103, 107
Lynsor, 36

Mack, 29
MADDUX: Caroline V., 47;
   Doreas, 47; Jane E., 47;
   Mary Louisa, 47
Madison, 10; James, 76
Magdaline, 84
Magdelina, 40
Magdeline, 40
Mahala, 17, 18, 20, 22, 41, 72,
   73, 82, 83, 84
Mahaly, 20
Mahlen, 77
Major, 110
Malinda, 3, 5, 64
Malvina, 20, 36, 38, 58, 59, 92,
   99, 114
Malvinia, 20, 59
Malviny, 9
Manda, 119
Mann: John, 30; Mildred, 30;
   Rush, 30; Thomas, 30;
   Westwood, 30; Wilford, 30
Manuel, 24, 26, 30, 49, 52, 71,
   91, 107, 109
MANYETT: Antoni, 114
Mardula, 106
Margaret, 1, 2, 3, 5, 11, 12, 18,
   19, 25, 26, 41, 42, 47, 48, 49,
   64, 67, 71, 72, 73, 77, 82, 83,
   84, 85, 91, 94, 102, 103, 105
Margaret Ann, 76
Margery, 29
Maria, 1, 2, 3, 4, 6, 9, 10, 11,
   17, 19, 20, 22, 25, 26, 31, 34,
   37, 39, 40, 42, 47, 48, 49, 52,
   57, 58, 59, 62, 63, 64, 65, 66,

68, 69, 70, 71, 72, 76, 77, 79,
   80, 81, 82, 83, 84, 85, 89, 90,
   91, 92, 93, 94, 95, 96, 99,
   101, 103, 104, 105, 106, 107,
   109, 110, 113, 115, 116, 117,
   118, 119, 120
Maria Parker, 92
Maria Penker, 95
Maria Robinson, 62
Mariah, 8, 19, 24, 27, 28, 29,
   33, 34, 39, 41, 47, 60, 85
Marion, 79
Mark, 4, 30, 52, 57
Markannaby, 2
MARR: John Q., 117
Marsh Farm Estate, 4
Marshall, 1, 2, 7, 8, 9, 15, 18,
   20, 22, 25, 39, 54, 55, 57, 58,
   68, 81, 83, 84, 96, 104, 105,
   117; Catharine, 21
MARSHALL: A.A., 68; A.I.,
   69; Henry M., 64; I., 69;
   J.A., 68, 69; James, 119;
   James K., 113; James M., 6;
   Jaquilin, 37; John, 65; Mary
   E., 49; Munford, 24, 57, 82;
   William C., 115
Martha, 1, 2, 4, 5, 7, 8, 10, 17,
   18, 19, 20, 23, 27, 37, 38, 39,
   42, 47, 48, 51, 54, 55, 58, 59,
   63, 65, 67, 68, 69, 70, 71, 75,
   76, 79, 81, 82, 84, 85, 89, 99,
   101, 102, 105, 110, 111, 115,
   118
Martha Ann, 84, 85
Martha Brigs, 85
Martha Bumbey, 53
Martha Burress, 92
Martha Jane, 101
Marthey, 117
Martillison, 41
Martin, 7, 27, 42, 57, 58, 59,
   68, 69, 91, 99, 100, 114, 121
MARTIN: Charles, 51, 75, 78,
   90, 93, 101, 108, 120; Elias,

112

38, 39, 63; Elizabeth, 37; George, 39; George W., 63; Henry C., 37; Jno, 63; John, 39, 55; Margaret, 37; Mary, 63; Peyton D., 39; William E., 39, 63

Martin Jr., 98, 99

Martin Robinson, 95

Martin Sr., 98

Martin Williams, 95

Mary, 2, 3, 4, 5, 6, 8, 9, 10, 12, 15, 18, 19, 20, 22, 23, 24, 25, 26, 27, 29, 30, 33, 36, 37, 39, 41, 42, 46, 49, 51, 54, 55, 56, 57, 58, 59, 61, 65, 66, 67, 68, 69, 70, 71, 72, 75, 76, 78, 80, 81, 82, 84, 85, 86, 87, 88, 89, 90, 92, 93, 94, 95, 97, 99, 100, 101, 103, 104, 105, 107, 108, 110, 111, 113, 114, 115, 117, 118, 119, 120, 121

Mary Ann, 4, 10, 22, 38, 39, 41, 47, 48, 58, 59, 64, 68, 69, 84, 85, 89, 93, 103

Mary Ann Picket, 85

Mary Clow, 64

Mary Daniel, 65

Mary Elisa, 10

Mary Elizabeth, 40, 107

Mary Ellen, 37

Mary Fletcher, 92, 94

Mary Jackson, 92

Mary Jane, 3, 6, 21, 23, 31, 44, 65, 71, 85, 88, 89, 104, 107, 111

Mary Laura, 102

Mary Matt, 64

Mary Matthews, 117

Mary Pin, 101

Mary Turner, 11, 12

Maryann, 7, 24

Mason, 10, 42, 45, 60, 64, 67, 97; Betsy, 94; Edward, 30; Elizabeth, 30

MASON: Seth, 23

MASSIE: J.B., 69; Nimrod, 94

Matilda, 3, 4, 7, 8, 10, 19, 20, 23, 29, 34, 40, 51, 58, 59, 60, 65, 68, 69, 75, 81, 82, 88, 90, 93, 95, 98, 101, 102, 103, 108, 109, 111, 120

Matilda Picket, 85

Matt, 66, 120; Mary, 64

Matthew, 38, 95

Matthews: Mary, 117

Maud, 5

Maury, 21

Mauzy: John, 92

McCARTER: Rob, 39

McCLANAHAN: Elizabeth, 17; Emily, 8; John, 8, 48, 97

McClintock: Jesse, 21

McCONCHIE: William A., 41

McCORMICK: Elizabeth, 26; Hugh, 20; John, 26; Mary, 39; William, 35, 38, 39, 51; William William, 38

McCOY, 2; Alice C., 2; Charles W.C., 2; Delia, 2; Hezekiah, 2, 12, 26; John, 2; Leonard H., 2, 82; Lewis H., 2

McDONALD: I.W., 69; Thomas, 68, 69

McINTEERS: Lydia S., 63, 64

McKENNIE: Beverly, 119; Marcellus, 119; Mary, 119; Matthew, 119

MEADE: Frances B., 23; John N., 23; R.K., 23

Medora, 103

Meglin, 83

Melinda, 1, 58, 59, 70, 98, 102

Melissa, 22, 41

MELLON: W., 85; W.P., 48; W.R., 81

Melvilla, 37

Melvin, 2, 88, 90

Melvina, 104

Mema Brent, 79

MENEFEE: Banks S., 95, 104, 115, 121
Meredith, 18, 20, 85
MEREDITH: Elizabeth, 105
Meshach, 16
Meshack, 16, 37, 41, 75, 78
Metallie, 117
Mias, 83
Michael, 17, 20, 66
MIDDLETON: Thomas, 51
Mike, 50, 95
Mikiel Thomson, 85
Mildred, 1, 8, 18, 20, 48, 65, 67, 83, 84, 85, 94, 114
Miles, 18, 120
Miller, 69; Henry, 46, 91, 115
Millon: Henry, 63
Mills, 120
Milly, 2, 3, 5, 11, 15, 17, 18, 19, 21, 25, 29, 33, 34, 39, 41, 45, 58, 59, 61, 62, 64, 65, 68, 69, 72, 75, 76, 78, 81, 84, 87, 92, 97, 109, 120
Milly Ann, 42
Milly Carter, 95
Milly Penker, 95
Milly Warner, 62
Milly Washington, 92
Milton, 57
Milton Taylor, 92
Mima, 36, 56
Mimy, 53, 99
Minerva, 89, 95
Minor, 12, 21
Minta, 7, 41, 99
Minty, 101, 111
Mira, 93
Miriam, 103
MITCHELL: Elizabeth M., 36; John, 30; Judith, 105
MITCHELL, Sr.: John, 34, 42
Mitt, 64
Molly, 2, 4, 7, 24, 34, 37, 39, 47, 48, 99, 117
Molly Lomax, 62

Monk, 84, 97
Montley, 19
MOORE: John, 15
MOREHEAD: A.H., 31; James, 8, 31
Morelin, 20
Morgan, 6, 53
MORGAN: Anna H., 64; Caroline W., 64; Charles, 69; George A., 68, 92; George L., 69; James, 64; Joseph, 52, 58, 59, 68; Josephine M.E., 38; Mary E., 79; Samuel Skinker, 64; William J., 65
Moro: Abner, 10
Morris, 49
MORRIS: Philip B., 104
MORRISON: Mary F., 31; Polly, 31, 34
MORSON: Maria M., 18
Morton, 52, 55
Moses, 10, 16, 18, 20, 22, 25, 28, 31, 36, 42, 44, 45, 52, 53, 61, 69, 71, 73, 80, 81, 82, 87, 93, 94, 98, 101, 103, 104, 109
Moses Bumbey, 53
Moses S__ell, 67
Moto, 101
Murray, 107
MURRAY: Alfred, 76, 98, 99, 100; James E., 100
Musket, 109
Myers, 84

Nace, 42, 84, 107
Nanchary, 20
Nancy, 2, 3, 5, 9, 10, 12, 19, 20, 23, 26, 29, 33, 36, 37, 41, 43, 47, 48, 53, 58, 64, 66, 68, 69, 78, 80, 84, 88, 96, 97, 106, 111
Nancy Elliott, 109
Nancy Keith, 89

114

Philander, 23
Philip, 119
PHILIPS: Caroline, 104; Elizabeth S., 104; Jno P., 104; John P., 114; Levinia R., 104; Philip B., 104
Phillip, 8, 68
Phillip Carter, 79
PHILLIPS: John P., 121; Philip B., 121; Victoria E., 121; W. Wesley, 114; William F., 21; William Wesley, 68, 105
Phillis, 58, 59, 68, 69, 72, 84, 99, 103
Phillis Tansel, 85
Phily, 55
Phoebe, 44
Phoebe James, 89
Picket: Caroline, 85; Mary Ann, 85; Matilda, 85
PICKETT: George, 42; James S., 38, 50; P.S., 39
PIERCE: M., 78
PILCHER: A.L., 68; Armistead T., 67; Catherine E., 67; Daniel, 52, 67; Daniel F., 67; Peter L., 67
Pin: Mary, 101
Pleasants: Eliza, 110
Polk, 19, 95
Polly, 2, 5, 7, 9, 11, 15, 16, 22, 23, 27, 28, 30, 34, 36, 38, 39, 41, 45, 48, 50, 52, 53, 62, 70, 79, 85, 91, 94, 95, 101, 109, 113, 118
Polly Cook, 23
Polly Mary, 6
Pompey, 33
PORTER, 37; Agnes, 20, 21, 28; John, 19; Lewis, 19, 21, 44; Martin, 19; Mary, 19, 46, 53, 62; Samuel, 19, 44; William, 19
Presley, 22, 72, 84

PRIEST: James, 34; Lucy, 68; Mary Ann, 9; Mason, 10
PRIMM: John, 110, 113
Prince, 5, 92, 99
Priscilla, 98
Priss, 25, 83

Quesenberg, 119
Quintus, 4, 10

Rachel, 3, 9, 10, 11, 12, 22, 31, 33, 44, 83, 88, 89, 95, 97, 99, 106, 109
Rachel Ann, 109
Rachel Bumbey, 53
Raleigh, 58, 59
Ralph, 4, 48, 105
Ralph Cummings, 48
Randall, 16, 22, 25, 28, 36, 45, 51, 53, 61, 75, 90, 93, 108, 120
Randolph, 110
RANDOLPH: Robert L., 84
Ransdell, 75
RANSDELL: Mary, 55; Mary C., 80; Mary E., 29
RAWLINGS: John D., 95, 120
Rebecca, 23, 58, 59, 68, 69
RECTOR: E., 107; Harriet, 104; Pratt, 94; Spencer, 56; Thomas A., 12; W., 68; William, 68, 78
REDD: Virginia, 83
REED: Henry, 47
Reid: Harry, 114
Remus, 2, 89
Reuben, 2, 12, 21, 22, 23, 26, 30, 38, 39, 48, 79, 91, 109
Reuben Roberts, 48
Rice, 52, 55
RICE: John S., 119, 121
Rice Payne, 63
Richard, 19, 22, 27, 29, 30, 40, 42, 45, 47, 49, 52, 56, 58, 59, 62, 63, 66, 68, 70, 71, 80, 83,

117

88, 90, 91, 97, 98, 99, 110, 115, 116
Richard Davis, 79
Richard William, 5
Richardetta, 50
RICHARDS: Elizabeth A., 11; Elizabeth I., 12; Emaline, 82, 86; Sarah M., 11, 12; Thompson, 3; Thompson H., 10, 12
RICKETTS: John, 44, 79
RIXEY: B.F., 8
Rob, 9
Robera Warner, 116
Robert, 2, 3, 6, 9, 15, 18, 22, 23, 25, 28, 30, 34, 39, 42, 47, 50, 52, 57, 60, 62, 63, 64, 69, 80, 81, 85, 87, 90, 93, 95, 97, 100, 105, 117
Robert D., 90
Robert Ferguson, 95
Roberta, 19, 20, 23, 40, 71, 77, 102, 107, 108, 120
Roberts: Aaron, 48; George, 48; John, 48; Reuben, 48; Sam, 48; Samuel, 48
Robertson, 29
Robin, 26, 29
Robinson: Maria, 62; Martin, 95; Otway, 62
ROBINSON: Agnes, 98; Ann Elizabeth, 38; Hannah, 1; John G., 54
ROBISON: Agnes, 61
Robuster, 2
ROE: Henry, 5; William, 5
ROGERS: Elizabeth, 116; Hugh, 56; Susannah, 87, 88
Rolla, 68, 69
Rollo, 52
Rolly, 30, 41, 50, 64
Rosa, 71
Rosalina, 41
Rosanna, 10, 40

Rose, 4, 5, 17, 20, 21, 29, 42, 49, 68, 69, 71, 75, 82, 83, 84, 86, 93, 95, 102, 104, 109, 120
ROSE: Mary Jane, 48; Mary S.H., 48; Mary Seym_ Hall, 45; Robert H., 48; William A., 45, 48
Rose Ann, 20
Rose Watson, 85
Rosella, 40, 51
Rosetta, 40, 49, 58, 59, 82, 103
Rosser, 33
Rosy, 7
Roszee, 7
Rowzee, 7
Roy, 8, 99
RUSSELL: Samuel, 113
RYAN: Maria C., 112
Ryland, 50

S__ell: Moses, 67
Sabrie, 55
Saby, 30
Sallery Davis, 110
Sally, 4, 11, 24, 25, 35, 37, 38, 42, 47, 50, 54, 57, 58, 59, 60, 61, 65, 66, 67, 71, 81, 82, 84, 85, 91, 94, 95, 97, 102, 103, 104, 112, 113, 114, 119
Sally Billy, 28
Sam, 2, 4, 7, 10, 12, 19, 22, 23, 30, 34, 38, 39, 42, 52, 55, 57, 58, 59, 63, 65, 71, 77, 81, 95, 96, 97, 99, 100, 106, 107, 108, 111, 120
Sam Roberts, 48
Sampson, 6, 18, 20, 29
Samson, 31
Samuel, 2, 3, 21, 22, 23, 30, 33, 34, 39, 63, 67, 80, 96, 97, 98, 105, 117
Samuel Jordan, 48
Samuel Jr., 39
Samuel Roberts, 48

118

Sanders, 4
SANDERS: Addison H., 49; Edward N., 49; Elijah Colman, 49; John A., 49; Judith, 49
Sandy, 7, 8, 17, 29, 40, 49, 67, 80, 87, 88, 92, 99, 108, 109, 111, 116
Sanford, 2, 22, 68, 69
Sara, 81
Sarah, 3, 8, 11, 12, 17, 20, 22, 23, 24, 37, 41, 42, 50, 52, 54, 56, 58, 59, 60, 64, 65, 67, 68, 71, 72, 75, 76, 84, 88, 95, 98, 101, 107, 111, 117, 120
Sarah Ann, 8, 20, 40, 94, 97, 105
Sarah Ann Lightfoot, 92
Sarah Catherine, 71
Sarah Frances, 40, 58, 59, 68, 69
Sarah Jane, 11, 12, 85
Sarale, 103
Sarale Francis, 103
Sary, 33, 109
Sary Frances, 11
Sathey, 3
Saunders, 10
SAUNDERS: George W., 47; Margaret, 47; Sarah, 60
Sawney, 65
SAYRES: Ann, 93
SCHENCK: Henry F., 49
Scike, 99
Scott, 38, 39, 65; John, 89; Lucy, 85
SCOTT: Betsy Blackwell, 18; John, 18, 42, 54; Robert E., 42, 114, 115, 120
Scylla, 99
Scyntha, 85
SEANLAND: Daniel, 34
SEATON: James P., 41, 45, 63, 75, 76; Mrs. E.F., 45
Seddon: Lewis, 80

Seinea, 29
Selma, 65
Seth, 61, 73, 82
Seven, 28, 43, 50, 77, 80
SHACKELFORD: Walker, 80
Shad, 37
Shadrack, 16, 36, 37, 41, 45, 64, 66, 67, 75, 78, 80, 94, 95, 97, 98, 99, 100, 106, 109
Shadrick, 37
Shake, 37
Shakespear, 37
SHAMBLIN, 77
Shapley, 47
Sharlotte, 52
SHEARMAN: George W., 51; Thomas, 51, 76; Thomas M., 51
Shelton, 88
Shingles, 30
SHIP: Charles R.S., 8; Ellen S., 8; Henrietta Clay, 8; John, 8, 10
SHORT: Julia, 81; Juliet, 11
SHUMATE: Bailey, 3; John W., 108; Joseph, 9; Lewis, 39, 63, 106, 107
Sidney, 57, 79, 84, 89, 95, 107
Silas, 6, 12, 17, 18, 19, 20, 33, 51, 52, 58, 59, 62, 75, 80, 90, 93, 101, 108, 120
Silva, 27, 83
Silvia, 54
Silvy, 21, 37
Simms, 84
Simon, 1, 4, 6, 7, 10, 38, 39, 59, 96, 97, 98, 101
Simon Peter, 119
SIMPSON: John F., 56
Sinah, 15, 28, 78
Sinai, 61, 95
SINCLAIR: C., 104; Charity, 72; James A., 1; Rosamond, 72
Sintha, 1

119

Sisily, 1, 3
SKINKER: James K., 8; William, 4
Sman, 28
Smith, 84, 95, 106; Arthur, 92
SMITH: _.W., 45; Agnes C., 77; Anderson D., 116; Angelina, 111; Ann D., 111; Benjamin F., 78; Eleanor, 1, 24; Elijah, 107, 118; Elizabeth, 25, 109; Enoch D., 110; George S., 111, 121; George W., 27; George W.E., 47; Hedgman, 110; Hugh G., 33; Isaac E., 78; James G., 110; John, 48, 111, 118; John A.W., 11; John J., 27; John P., 109; Lucy, 78; M.C., 87; Maria C., 33; Mary A., 89; Mary Ann, 88; Mary F., 111; Mary H., 103; Mildred, 109; P.G., 69; Sally, 85, 97; Susan V., 109; Thomas, 109; Thomas D., 34; Thomas W., 24, 36, 70; Thomas Williamson, 21; W.A., 25; Walter A., 24; Wilfred A., 25; William, 50, 61; William J., 46; William R., 66, 77, 78
SMITH Sr.: Thomas W., 45
SMOOT: Daniel James, 39
Snelling: George, 44
Snowden, 102
Solomon, 18, 20, 28, 50, 57, 58, 59, 68, 69, 93, 95
Sommerville, 93
Sophia, 1, 17, 20, 30, 35, 40, 57
Sophie, 6, 50
Sophy, 17, 58, 59, 68, 113
South, 104
Sowers: Florinza, 92
SOWERS: Robert _.W., 56; William, 47; William H., 56
Spence, 39

SPENCE: Mary, 36
Spencer, 2, 4, 11, 12, 15, 21, 22, 26, 34, 49, 57, 58, 59, 63, 81, 85, 88, 95, 104, 114, 117
Spencer Butler, 48
Spencer White, 57
SPILLMAN: Jane, 93; Susan, 56
SPINDLE: Sarah, 111; William, 111
Squire, 42, 94
STANTON: John C., 110; Thomas T., 110
Stanton G., 90
Staunton, 95, 103
Stephanie, 92
Stephen, 19, 23, 24, 31, 49, 58, 59, 63, 68, 69, 84, 89, 97, 107, 117, 119
Stephen Brent, 79
STEPHENS: Alexander, 48; Elizabeth, 70; James H., 70
Stephner, 99
STEWART: Eliza, 68; Emily, 72; Harriet, 6; Nancy B., 72; Stephen A., 10; William, 1
STIGLER, 114, 115; Alice, 27; James, 27
Stilby, 9
STONE: Anne, 53; Jno, 47
STOVER: Magga, 104
STRIBLING: Caroline M., 111; Robert M., 111; William C., 112
STRINGFELLOW: James, 5
Strother, 24, 31, 43, 48, 103, 104; Jesse, 62; Nancy, 62
STROTHER: Ann M., 99; C.M., 99; Catherine Mildred, 41; James, 99, 106; John, 113; Lewis, 7; Mary, 2, 3, 4, 24; Nancy, 7; Susannah, 56
Strother Bennley, 44
Strother Butler, 48

120

Stuart: Charles, 92; Jenny, 92; Violet, 92
STUART: Helen, 3; William, 16, 26
Suck, 5
Suckey, 23
SUDDOTH: Elizabeth A., 26; Harriet, 85; J.T., 69; James T., 69; Joseph, 47; Margaret, 85; Mary B., 85
Sue, 70
Sukey, 26
Sukey Jr., 103
Sulkey, 66
Sullivan, 120
SULLIVAN: Ann Eliza, 102; Emily Scrivener, 102; James Bailey, 102; James R., 102; John, 56, 109; John H., 102; Luther O., 102; Mary, 102; Owen, 22, 102; Wade, 102; Willis, 56
SUMMER: Sarah C., 28
Summerfield, 95
SUMMERS: Lucy C., 89; Lucy Catlet, 88
Summerville, 49, 61, 80, 87
SUNCEFORD: K., 23
Susan, 3, 4, 6, 8, 10, 18, 20, 22, 24, 27, 29, 33, 39, 41, 42, 44, 45, 47, 48, 49, 52, 54, 56, 58, 60, 63, 65, 76, 77, 78, 79, 89, 90, 91, 95, 96, 97, 98, 100, 101, 103, 104, 107, 112, 113, 116, 117, 119
Susan Ann, 84
Susan Jackson, 92
Suzy, 15
Swane, 50
SWART: William R., 106, 107
Sydner, 69
Sydney, 25, 78
Sydney Maria, 25
Sydnor, 13, 42, 48, 51, 60, 67, 78, 91

Sylva, 60, 69, 70, 85
Sylvia, 42, 47, 55, 63, 72
Sylvinus, 58, 59, 68
Sylvy, 106

T_onssle, 22
Tabby, 71
Talbert: Alex, 48
Taliaferro, 52, 58, 59, 68, 69, 75
Tally, 101
Tama, 37, 97
Tamar, 65, 92
Tamer Butler, 92
Tansel: Phillis, 85
TAPP: Elizabeth H., 49, 61; Mildred, 49
Tarleton, 3, 9
Taylor, 27, 39, 54; Allison, 92; Emily, 92; Felix, 92; James Henry, 92; Lizza, 92; Lucy, 89; Milton, 92; Thornton, 92
Taylor Jackson, 92
Tazwell, 94
TEBBS: Betsy, 37, 43; Elizabeth, 36; Samuel, 36; Thomas T., 36; Tonshew, 36
Tempe, 61
Teresa, 18, 20
Thaddeus, 47, 63, 70, 83, 115
Thadius, 27
Thom, 70
THOM: Ada M., 95, 97
Thomas, 1, 10, 22, 25, 27, 30, 37, 39, 42, 47, 48, 52, 58, 59, 64, 76, 78, 97, 99, 103, 107, 118
THOMAS: John, 4
Thomas George, 21
Thomas Hove, 66
Thomas Jr., 85
Thomas Sr., 85
THOME: W.N., 68, 69
Thompson, 45, 66

THOMPSON, 114; C.H., 91, 114, 115; Clark H., 83; Clarke, 115, 116; Clarke H., 70, 91, 115; Dr. William, 16; John J., 48; Joseph, 27, 36, 46, 47, 63, 70, 82, 83, 91, 115, 116; Joseph W., 48; Mary Ann, 48; Mary E., 46; William A,, 53; William A., 48, 50

Thomson: Frederick, 92; Mikiel, 85

THOMSON: John W., 109

Thornton, 3, 7, 8, 10, 12, 15, 18, 20, 39, 47, 50, 53, 60, 61, 64, 65, 66, 76, 78, 80, 93, 94, 95, 101, 102, 103, 116

Thornton Taylor, 92

TIBBS, Jr: Charles B., 34

TIDBALL: Alex S., 23; E.M., 23; Josiah, 7, 23; Lucy, 7; Lucy G., 23; Milicent, 23

TIETT: James, 78

TIFFANY: Sarah, 106

Tim, 5, 6, 10, 12

TIMBERLAKE: John, 87

TIMBERLAKE Jr.: William, 51

Tina, 113

Titus, 94

Tol, 120

Tolbert: Ben, 3

Toliver, 51, 75, 90, 101, 120

TOLSON: Mary Adalaide, 21

Tom, 2, 4, 6, 7, 15, 16, 19, 23, 26, 34, 37, 40, 48, 52, 54, 57, 58, 59, 61, 66, 67, 68, 69, 71, 76, 78, 79, 83, 84, 85, 92, 94, 95, 103, 104, 108, 109, 114, 118

Tom Turner, 70

TOMLIN: Hannah, 20; Sarah, 20; Stephen, 20

TOMPSON: Susan, 20

Tomsom, 66

Tony, 2, 22, 34, 39, 57

Townsend, 85

Townson, 24

TRACEY: Lewis, 110

Tracy, 4

Travis, 100, 102

TRENT: Hugh, 50; Jno M., 68

TREVERLEY: Robert, 48

TRIPLETT: L., 78; Margaret, 36; Nathaniel, 101; Susan, 101; Thomas, 116

Tristan, 51

Troy, 80

Truston, 22

TUCKER: William A., 111

Tulip, 50, 119

TULLOSS: Joseph I., 47; R.G., 46, 67; William H., 67

Turner, 67, 69, 81, 85, 90, 94, 97, 101, 120; Alfred, 97; Mary, 11

TURNER: Edward C., 27; Eliza C., 116; Henry H., 54; Sarah, 15; Thomas, 116

Tyler, 50, 60; Elizabeth, 89; Henrietta, 89

TYLER: Jno W., 121; John W., 108; Mrs., 40; Randolph, 108

Unity, 87

Ursley, 88, 90

UTTERBACK: Byrant, 8; French, 72, 85, 99; Joseph, 8; Nathanial, 100; OBannon, 8; Porter, 8, 100, 109; Wilford, 8, 54; William, 5, 8, 22; William J., 105

VASS: Susan, 113

Venice, 29

Venus, 113

Vernon Butler, 92

Vianna, 11, 67, 94

Vic, 70

Victoria, 27, 63, 83, 91, 115, 116
Vienna, 12, 41
Vina, 71, 77, 103, 104
Vincent, 16, 22, 25, 28, 36, 45, 53, 61, 97, 104, 106
Viney, 3, 5, 18, 57
Violet, 1, 5, 26, 30, 48, 68, 82, 86, 92, 97
Violet Stuart, 92
VIOLETT: Ashford, 25
Virginia, 2, 7, 18, 20, 30, 34, 38, 40, 55, 80, 120

W_OL_ESTRN: Samuel, 47
Wade, 113
Wager, 79; Henry, 90
Walford, 2, 27
Walker, 58, 59, 68, 69, 71, 101; Lucy, 62
WALKER: Mrs., 89
Wallace, 40, 58, 59, 62, 68, 87, 88, 89, 108, 109, 115, 116
WALLACE: Elizabeth M., 13; John, 66; John R., 13; Margaret H., 34; Mary, 66
Waller, 47, 63, 70, 77, 83, 91, 114, 115, 116
WALLER: Adeline, 29; Anne S., 112; Frances, 29; H., 56; Margaret, 29; Mary, 11; Susan, 29
Walter, 27
WALTON: Melvin N., 10; Mr., 2; Susan, 10
Wanser, 17, 19
Wanzo, 50
WARD: A.B., 103; Berkely, 103; Berkley, 103; Fitzhugh, 103; Henry Clay, 103; John, 103; Mrs. K., 103; Susan M., 103; William, 107
Warden, 47
WARDER: Elizabeth A., 81
Wardon, 48

Warner, 40, 66, 79, 107, 117; Annie Moore, 116; Daniel, 116; Fanny, 116; Jannette, 116; Judy, 62; Milly, 62; Robera, 116
Warrenton, 84
Wash, 95, 101
Washington, 4, 7, 10, 25, 40, 51, 58, 59, 66, 68, 69, 72, 75, 81, 90, 93, 108; Aaron, 92; Clara, 92; Cornelia, 92; Eli, 92; George, 92; Milly, 92
WASHINGTON, 114; John A., 117; John A., 107
WATERS: Jonathan, 39; Mary, 106
Watson: Rose, 85
Waverly Corum, 92
WEAVER, 3; Alfred A., 3; Ann G., 49; Charles A., 3; Chrisitana E., 81; Christiana A., 81; Elizabeth S., 3; Jacob M., 3; Janet C., 100; Joseph, 37, 62; Lavinia G., 3; Margaret, 3; Margaret A.et, 60; Mary, 3; Ocatvius A., 3; Oscar, 3; R.A., 81; Samuel, 81; William S., 3, 49; William T., 81
WEAVER, Jr: Joseph, 3
Webster, 76
Weedon, 31
WEEDON: John Isaac, 53; Lucetta, 53; Rebecca, 53, 56; Rebecca Elizabeth Anne, 53; Thomas W., 53
WEEKS: Mary, 40
WELCH: Sylvester, 46, 47
Welk: Harry, 17
Wellford Butler, 92
WELLINGHAM: A., 69
Wellington, 25, 72, 119
Wesley, 4, 19, 20, 29, 45, 51, 58, 59, 65, 68, 69, 71, 75, 78, 80, 87, 90, 93, 101, 108, 120

West, 3, 115, 120
WEST: Benjamin, 53; Elizabeth, 53
Westley, 29
WHEATLEY: Susan, 5, 18; W.I., 68; William I., 69
WHITE: Ann Eliza, 34; Augustine M., 34; Daniel, 24; George, 24; Harriet, 11; James, 20, 24, 34; James A., 34; Jno T., 24; Obid, 24, 52; Obid M., 34; Robb, 113; William, 24, 81
WHITING: James S., 25
WILCHER: Jno, 69
Wiley, 51, 76
Wilford, 6, 18, 20, 39, 57, 81, 104, 117
Wilfred, 56, 97
Will, 48
William, 2, 5, 6, 7, 9, 11, 12, 17, 19, 21, 23, 24, 25, 27, 29, 30, 33, 35, 37, 40, 41, 42, 43, 45, 47, 48, 49, 50, 51, 52, 54, 55, 57, 62, 64, 66, 67, 71, 73, 75, 80, 81, 82, 83, 84, 85, 86, 87, 88, 89, 90, 92, 93, 94, 95, 96, 97, 98, 99, 100, 101, 103, 104, 105, 108, 110, 119
WILLIAM: Rosalis, 113
William Brooke, 95
William Grant, 27, 47, 63, 70, 83, 114
William Henry, 30, 31, 37, 41, 45, 59, 84
William Henry Burress, 92
William Henry H., 40
William Jeff, 47, 63, 70, 83, 115
William Jones, 41, 45
William Smith, 74
Williams: Martin, 95
WILLIAMSON: Rev. William, 9; T._., 22; William, 3, 22
Willie, 93, 114, 115

Willie Ann Corum, 92
Willis, 3, 5, 15, 38, 39, 47, 57, 60, 64, 72, 85, 92, 95, 99, 107, 111
WILLIS: Jno P., 121; John P., 100; Maria, 113; Matilda, 87; Peyton E., 87
Willoughby, 4, 17, 31, 61, 77
Willy Ann, 106
Wilson, 4, 30, 52; George, 42
WILSON: Archibald, 8; Jno A., 105
Wilson Ball, 85
Windsor, 119
WINGFIELD: John J., 114; Thomas S., 114
Winifred, 22
Winnie, 80, 99
Winny, 4, 7, 8, 11, 15, 19, 21, 26, 38, 39, 49, 70, 71, 84, 85, 106, 110
Winter, 105
WITHERS: Agnes, 21, 98; Agnes A., 108; Andrew, 9; Andrew T., 9; Bettie S., 9; Elizabeth S., 9; Horace C., 25; Horatio C., 9; Jesse H., 5, 91, 104, 109; Jessie H., 71; Sally, 5; Thomas T., 110; Thornton, 21
WOLFE Jr.: A., 78
WOLFE Sr.: A., 78
Wood: John, 109
WOOD: Eliza, 102
WOOLF: A., 94; Andrew, 93, 94; Ann, 9; H.M., 94
WOUGH: Tabitha A., 18
WRIGHT: William B., 60
WYCKOFF: William, 5, 30

Yancy, 17
YERBY: William G., 114

Zachariah, 72, 76, 97
Zachary, 95

124

Zack, 81

www.ingramcontent.com/pod-product-compliance
Lightning Source LLC
Chambersburg PA
CBHW070252290326
41930CB00041B/2462